Feast
of
Stephen

Feast of Stephen

A Cornucopia of Delights
by Stephen Leacock
Selected and Introduced
by Robertson Davies

M&S

The selections in this edition have been taken from a variety
of editions, Canadian, British, and American.
Spelling and style of the source editions have been retained.

Acknowledgement is made to:

Doubleday Inc. for permission to reprint "Life on the Old
Farm" from THE BOY I LEFT BEHIND ME; Dodd, Mead
& Co., Inc. for permission to reprint "Impervious to Women"
from HAPPY STORIES and "Education Eating Up Life"
from TOO MUCH COLLEGE; The Stephen Leacock Estate
for permission to reprint "The Hero of Home Week" and
"Mr. Chairman, I Beg to Move" from THE IRON MAN AND
THE TIN WOMAN.

The introduction is available in a slightly different version in
a paperback entitled *Stephen Leacock,* by Robertson Davies.

Canadian Cataloguing in Publication Data

Leacock, Stephen, 1869-1944.
    Feast of Stephen: a cornucopia of delights

Includes bibliographical references.
ISBN 0-7710-2577-7

I. Davies, Robertson, 1913-   II. Title.

PS8523.E15F4 1990   C818′.5207   C90-095284-9
PR9199.2.L42F4 1990

Printed and bound in Canada

McClelland & Stewart Inc.
The Canadian Publishers
481 University Avenue
Toronto, Ontario M5G 2E9

Table of Contents

Introduction

1

In a letter which he wrote in 1890 to the influential critic Andrew Lang, Mark Twain had this to say:

> The little child is permitted to label its drawings "This is a cow — this is a horse" and so on. This protects the child. It saves it from the sorrow and wrong of hearing its cows and its horses criticized as kangaroos and work-benches. A man who is whitewashing a fence is doing a useful thing, so also is the man who is adorning a rich man's house with costly frescoes; and all of us are sane enough to judge these performances by standards proper to each. Now then, let us be fair to an author who ought to be allowed to put upon his book an explanatory line: "This is written for the Belly and the Members." And the critic ought to hold himself in honour bound to put away from him his ancient habit of judging all books by one standard and thenceforth follow a fairer course. .... Yes, you see, I have always catered for the Belly and the Members, but have been served like the others – criticized by the culture-standard – to my sorrow and pain. .... And now at last I arrive at my object and tender my petition, making supplication to this effect: that the critics adopt a rule recognizing the Belly and the Members and formulate a standard whereby work done for them shall be judged.

Let us bear Mark Twain's plea in mind when considering the work of Stephen Butler Leacock, for if ever a man wrote for the Belly and the Members it was Leacock. But we must also remember that the comments of artists on their work, and their desire that it be judged in some particular manner, is a form of special pleading; what a man writes, if he is a serious writer, is very dear to him because it comes from what is deepest and most important in him. He cannot be any more objective than a mother who hears a neighbour say that her baby is ugly; to mothers there are no ugly babies. Nor is all work addressed to the Belly and the Members on the same

1

level; some of it is the durable work of genius, like the great fantasy of François Rabelais, and some is the blossom of a day, like the writings of Artemus Ward, regarded by Abraham Lincoln as very funny, but now out of fashion and not likely to be revived. When we talk of Leacock, we shall only make ourselves absurd if we dissect and paw his work as if it were, for instance, the painstaking composition of such a humorist as James Joyce. Leacock had a substantial vanity controlled by the upbringing of a Victorian gentleman and a man of classical learning, but he wrote for the largest mass audience he could command and he would have laughed at a critic who grew too serious about his work. Let us therefore keep a reasonable balance in our critical discussion and bear in mind at all times the character of the man we are considering.

There: that is one critical principle laid down already, and it may be one which will make some serious readers put this essay aside as of no account. For I have confessed that I mean to relate Stephen Leacock's personal character and biography to his work, and there are many who think that any such procedure must lead to bad criticism. They think the printed text all that may fairly be examined in a critical appraisal. With the works of some writers this may well be so, but with Leacock – or anybody who addresses himself to the Belly and the Members – I think not.

He wrote copiously, getting up early to put in two hours at his desk before the rest of his household was stirring. But he also wrote carelessly; his works abound with misquotations, misattributions and repetitions. He would get a brilliant idea, exploit it admirably, and then dismiss it with a lame conclusion, as in "A, B, and C" in *Literary Lapses.* I have no evidence that he admired the working methods of Anthony Trollope, or ever read the *Autobiography* where Trollope describes them, but he certainly employed the same principle. He demanded of himself a certain amount of writing, as did Trollope, and, like Trollope, he often wrote when he would have done better to sit still and wait for an idea. He admired industry and he admired method, but his best work is not the result of industry and method; these produced the thin and repetitious books of his mid-career. His best work was the outpouring of genius.

Yes; genius. Critics are hesitant about using this word, but if it means a capacity for imaginative creation so extraordinary as sometimes to rise above what can be produced by the conscious exertion of an unusually gifted man, that was what Leacock had. If, in the realm of writing, it means individuality so striking as to provoke the admiration, envy and imitation of men themselves finely gifted – as Robert Benchley handsomely admitted was the case between Leacock and himself – certainly Leacock had genius. But he did not treat himself as a genius; he did not even treat himself as a writer of distinction; he did not weed and select and try to repress work that was far below his best level. There was no pinch of poverty to drive him to his desk when he had nothing in particular to say, as has been the case with many a genius who has written a lot of inferior stuff. What drove him to write so much and to work so hard I cannot pretend to know, for he was reticent about his personal feelings, and so far no material has come to light that would tell us anything about the reason for his compulsive industry. We can but guess, and though I shall try to support any opinions I express on this matter with facts and deductions, they must remain guesses still.

2

Stephen Leacock was born at Swanmore, in Hampshire, on December 30, 1869; it is a tiny place, not to be found on ordinary maps, but it is a mile and a half from Bishop's Waltham, ten miles south-east of Winchester. For a time Leacock thought that his birthplace was Swanmore near Ryde in the Isle of Wight. How he settled the point is amusingly described in his unfinished, excellent autobiography, *The Boy I Left Behind Me*. He points out, also, that the year of his birth was the exact middle of Queen Victoria's reign. Because his parents moved to Canada in 1876, when he was six years old, his memories of life in Hampshire are few and touched with the charm of happiness warmly felt, though dimly recalled. But he does speak of the beauty of the splendid sailing-ships that still were to be seen at Portchester, and of an old sailor, known to him, who had fought in "the Great War," by which was meant the war against Napoleon.

He is facetious about his descent and quotes from a booklet about his family which contains what he calls "the fatal sentence," which is this: "The first recorded Leacock was a London day-labourer, whose son was brought up at a charity school and went out as a ship's cabin-boy to Madeira." But that cabin-boy must have gone to Madeira not later than the early years of the eighteenth century, and by the time Leacock was born, his name was well-known as that of a family in the wine trade on a large scale. They were not aristocratic, but they had enjoyed the ease and education of the upper middle-class for several generations. His mother's family, the Butlers, were of a somewhat superior social class – country gentry, indeed. Stephen Leacock was of privileged birth.

Do you know the characteristic wine of Madeira? Some of it is dry, and not unlike a heavy sherry; some of it is sweet, and rivals port as a fine dessert wine. But all of it has a curious aftertaste, much appreciated by connoisseurs, which is like brimstone, and is caused by the volcanic soil of the island. I

4

do not know whether Leacock ever drank Madeira himself
– he was very much a Scotch-whisky man – but I enjoy
Madeira greatly, and I never drink it without thinking of
Leacock, who was sometimes dry, sometimes sweet, but who
always leaves upon the tongue a hint of brimstone. His
amiability was great, but those who knew him have stories
of his sudden flashes of hot temper, of impatience and
irascibility. He wrote of his friend, Sir Andrew Macphail:

> I am certain that he never quite knew what he believed and
> what he didn't; but underneath it was a deep-seated feeling
> that the real virtue of a nation is bred in the country, that
> the city is an unnatural product. From this point of view
> Andrew, though frequenting the rich in his daily walk of
> life, was never quite satisfied of their right to be. Towards
> plutocrats, bankers, manufacturers and such, he felt a little
> bit as a rough country dog feels towards a city cat. He
> didn't quite accept them. Andrew would have made a fine
> radical if he hadn't hated radicalism.

In this description he might have been writing of himself.
Leacock was a lifelong professed Tory; he valued money and
was pleased by the big income his writings brought him. But
he never really seems to have liked rich people or aristocrats
and he never misses a chance to take a dig at them. Yet he,
like Bernard Shaw, came of a privileged class and, again like
Shaw, of a family that was down on its luck. Despite their
best efforts, neither of them ever really got over having been
born a gentleman. Leacock too would have made a fine
radical, but the hooligan element that attaches itself to
radicalism repelled him.

Leacock loved his mother dearly and came to hate his
father. Peter Leacock had been raised a Roman Catholic, but
it was in the Church of England (All Saints, Norfolk Square,
in London) that Agnes Emma Butler, daughter of an Anglican clergyman, Stephen Butler, married him in a runaway
match, and shortly afterward emigrated to South Africa.
They lasted there about a year, then returned to Hampshire,
where Peter tried his hand at farming. It was an uneasy time,
for the Papist father was never asked to the Anglican Butlers'
home. Having failed at farming in England, Peter formed
the idea, not uncommon among Englishmen of his type and
of his time, that he would succeed at it in Canada, and in
1876 the family went to a farm a few miles south of Lake
Simcoe near Sutton, in Ontario. Leacock described it as "the
damnedest place I ever saw." It was another failure. Peter

went to Winnipeg for the boom and came back after the bust. In 1887, when Stephen was seventeen, Peter went away for the last time. Ralph H. Curry records a story as from "a member of the family" that Stephen drove his father to the station at Sutton in the cutter, and picking up the buggy-whip said, "If you come back, I'll kill you." There's brimstone!

The Leacock family eventually numbered eleven children – of whom Stephen was the third – all of whom grew up on that ill-starred farm, in an atmosphere of debt and misery that their mother could not wholly conceal from them. He describes it as "a shadowed, tragic family life." The atmosphere of the neighbouring school was not suitable; little boys in School Section No. 3., Township of Georgina, used such expressions as "them there" and "these here." Let us not dismiss the objections of Agnes Leacock as snobbery; that kind of English would have held her boys back in the world. For a time she tried teaching them herself, but history is not rich in records of parents who have successfully educated their own offspring. A private tutor, one Harry Park, was engaged and proved a great success. And in 1882, when he was thirteen, Stephen followed his brothers Jim and Dick to Toronto, to Upper Canada College, where he completed his schooling and achieved the distinction of being Head Boy.

Leacock is careful to explain that Upper Canada was not a snob school; it was a place where families could send boys to get them out of the "them there" atmosphere of deeply rural schools. Nevertheless, there was a measure of pride inescapable by one who was a member of a first-rate school with a fine staff, and in his account of his school days he cannot avoid it. It was part of the struggle which lasted all his life, and on which he wasted so much time, to prove that although he was manifestly a man of uncommon abilities and substantial personal advantages, he was still just "plain folks." Doubtless this had much to do with his idea of himself as a widely popular humorist, a man who addressed himself to the Belly and the Members, but there was more to it than that.

It seems to have been part of a tension that was strong in his make-up, that made him deplore class distinctions while expecting people who had a good place in life to behave as though they believed in them; that made him contemptuous of aristocracy and a keen admirer of Washington and Jefferson, while personally supporting the monarchy and the Tory Party and making large claims for the British Empire; that made him strongly and even bitterly critical of classical education, advocating technical and scientific education as the hope of civilization, while relying on the discipline of a classical education to form his intellectual tastes. It may have been this tension between intellect and emotion, theory and experience, that made him a humorist. Tension must find its outlet somehow. In mediocre people, it may simply cause ill-temper, but a man of Leacock's powers would have had to become either a fanatic, crushing emotion in the service of theory, or a humorist, accepting the contradictions of his temperament without trying too strenuously to reconcile them. But intellectual tension is observable in much of his best and most characteristic work, and I shall have to refer to it often.

When he had finished school, what was to follow? He had no money to go to the University of Toronto save a scholarship of a hundred dollars, which his mother eked out to the requisite sum from her own income of eighty dollars a month. Tuition in those days cost forty dollars a year, and to this must be added three dollars a week for food and lodging in a boarding-house; washing came to twenty-five cents a week, and books cost about ten dollars a year; Leacock reckoned that it took three hundred dollars to see a student through the eight months of college. Because of his status as a scholarship holder, he was allowed to telescope the first two university years into one, but that left him with no degree and the necessity to earn money. So he did what so many ambitious young men did at that time; he took the three months of training that would qualify him as a high school teacher and got a job at Uxbridge, where his former tutor Harry Park was now the principal, as teacher of modern languages, at seven hundred dollars a year. In his second year in Uxbridge, he received an offer from Upper Canada College to teach there for the same salary, and after an impassioned plea to the Uxbridge trustees to release him, he took it. It meant that he could teach during the school day, and continue his university classes as best he might after hours. He was a schoolmaster in all for ten and a half years (February, 1889 until July, 1899) and disliked the work heartily.

In later life Leacock wrote often and disparagingly about the work of the school teacher. It seemed to him to be a dead end into which young men were trapped by the initial chance to make what looked like a good salary, but which lost its gloss as middle age approached, so that the aging teacher was a pitiable creature, short of cash and held in low esteem by the community. This opinion contrasts oddly with his good opinion of professors, whom he represents, in *Arcadian Adventures With the Idle Rich,* as unworldly but upright men, devoted to an ideal of truth in a continent corrupted by greed for money and luxury. But it is unfair to judge Leacock as if he were upon oath every time he took up his pen. The fact is, probably, that he hated the narrow life that a small salary and a subordinate position imposed on him when he was a teacher and he gloried in the freedom and authority of a professor. Like many other people – and it may be that they are the lucky ones – Leacock's best period came when youth had gone; not everybody is well-suited to being young, and certainly a man so opinionated and energetic as Leacock cannot have liked being a man under authority. The best of his life began in 1899 when, drawn by the chance of working with Thorstein Veblen, he enrolled as a graduate student at the University of Chicago; in 1900 he married Beatrix Hamilton; in 1903 he was awarded his Ph.D. in political economy and political science, *magna cum laude.* He already held the modest post of a sessional lecturer in these subjects at McGill. His feet were now firmly set on the path which was to be his through life.

It was a path of success, though he bore the blows of Fate every man encounters from time to time. His only child, born in 1915, had an affliction that impaired his growth; his wife's death, from cancer, in 1925, ended a marriage from which he had drawn great sustenance; his compulsory retirement from McGill at sixty-five – he had himself supported this ruling, at a time when doubtless sixty-five seemed far away – hurt him deeply, and he obviously thought the university should have made an exception of him. But he had a generous share of the sweets of life. Admiration and fame (they are not always linked) and money were his in substantial measure. He enjoyed the rewards of life and met the blows with stoicism. Of religious feeling, of a sense that a man's destiny may not be something he shapes entirely by himself, he seems to have felt nothing, and therefore stoicism was the path he took in misfortune.

He lived well, possessing a handsome Montreal house on Côte des Neiges Road, and his much-loved summer home (which he attempted, fitfully and unsuccessfully, to run as a farm) on Old Brewery Bay, on Lake Couchiching. In 1908 he was appointed William Dow Professor of Political Economy and, at the same time, chairman of the department of economics at McGill. It was in this year also that he and a group of colleagues founded the University Club of Montreal, which served him almost as a third home. He was a popular professor, a good and light-handed administrator, and came in time to be one of the world-famous ornaments of his university. He lectured widely on the North American continent, in England, and, under the auspices of the Cecil Rhodes Trust, he toured the British Empire as a lecturer in 1907-8, speaking on Imperial Organization; wherever he went, he carried the name of McGill with him, so there was some justice in his feeling that the university might have exempted him from its ruling about retirement. He received honorary degrees from Queen's University, Kingston, from Dartmouth, from Brown, from the University of Toronto, from Bishop's, Lennoxville, and, after his retirement, from McGill itself. On March 28, 1944, in Toronto, he died of cancer of the throat in his seventy-fifth year.

In this brief account of his life I have concentrated on his youth, rather than on the later and much longer period of his success and his fame, for I think that the disquiets and probably also the miseries of his family life, and the struggle against poverty, were the most important influences on him. Like Bernard Shaw, he had known genteel poverty and the necessity to maintain a certain social standing and cultural background on insufficient means. Like Shaw, he never forgot it; unlike Shaw, he appears to have allowed it to push him into paths unfriendly to his greatest development as a literary artist.

But does a man who addresses himself to the Belly and the Members think of himself as an artist? Toward the end of his life Leacock seems to have reached some such opinion.

3

In the preface to *How to Write*, Leacock says:

> I did not personally get started writing, except for a few odd pieces, until I was forty years old. Like the milkmaid with a fortune in her face, I had a fortune (at least as good as hers) in my head. Yet I spent ten weary years as an impecunious schoolmaster without ever realizing this asset. The fault, like that of Abdul the Bulbul Ameer, was "entirely my own." I had too little courage, was too sensitive. I had a little initial success with odd humorous writings in the early 'nineties. I can see now that the proportion of success I had was exceptionally high and that the rejection of a manuscript should have meant no more than a blow of a feather. Still more did I fail in not knowing where to find material for literary work. It seemed to me that my life as a resident schoolmaster was so limited and uninteresting that there was nothing in it to write about. Later on, when I had learned how, I was able to turn back to it and write it up with great pecuniary satisfaction. But that was after I had learned how to let nothing get past me. I can write-up anything now at a hundred yards.

There is a self-satisfaction about these words, addressed to people who want to learn something about writing, that tells us a good deal about Leacock, especially that last boast that he can "write-up anything at a hundred yards." There is nothing here of the shrinking violet; indeed, it is the self-assertive tone of the passage that makes it interesting. Leacock seems truly to have believed that he had perfected a technique for turning anything into his own kind of fun, and it is to this conviction that we must attribute the long stretches of mechanical joke-smithing that make the books of his mid-career wearisome reading today.

Perhaps this is the moment to say that lack of confidence never seems to have troubled Leacock after he obtained his McGill appointment. The late B. K. Sandwell once told me that it came in time to mar even his public appearances; he approached his audiences not – as he says in "We Have With Us To-Night" (in *My Discovery of England*) – "in his little white waistcoat and his long-tailed coat and with a false air of a conjuror about him," but with the condescension of one who seems to say, "I, the great Stephen Leacock, will now delight you." Leacock's vanity was a part of his forceful masculinity of which I shall write later. But the passage quoted at the beginning of this chapter, from a late and revealing book, tells us two things: Leacock began his career late, and he fell into the trap of thinking that he had mastered his art. In truth, only technique can be mastered; art masters those who serve it, in whatever form.

It was not art, but scholarship and exposition that brought about the success of his first book, *Elements of Political Science,* in 1906. It supplied a want in the university world, quickly achieved a wide sale in English, and before the exhaustion of its usefulness, it had been translated into nineteen languages; it was always Leacock's biggest money-maker. In 1907 he followed it with the volume *Baldwin, Lafontaine, Hincks: Responsible Government,* which was the fourteenth volume in the "Makers of Canada" series and very much in the author's line. It was not until these books had gained a flattering acceptance that he considered publishing a collection of his humorous pieces.

Leacock had been known among his friends as a wit from his college days; he was also a practical joker. The late Professor Keith Hicks, of Trinity College, Toronto, told me a story of a joke Leacock played on a fellow-master at U.C.C. who was apt to complain about his salary. He made the mistake of asking Leacock to draft a letter of protest to the Board of Governors, which in time was handed to him in this form: "Gentlemen: Unless you can see your way to increasing my stipend immediately, I shall reluctantly be forced to" – and here the page was turned – "continue working for the same figure." This is very good Leacock, for it demonstrates not only his wit but also his poorly disguised contempt for the world's incompetents, complainers, and no-hopers. Later he was to attempt to conceal this attitude, but he never wholly succeeded in doing so.

Curry tells us that Beatrix Leacock and Mrs. B. K. Sandwell assembled the collection of pieces that later bore the title of *Literary Lapses.* It was sent to Houghton Mifflin, who had published *Elements,* and they refused it, regarding funny books as a bad risk. It was Leacock's brother George who urged Stephen to publish the book himself, which he did in 1910; *The Gazette* printing company struck off 3000 copies, and The Montreal News Company marketed it as a "railway book" – the sort of thing sold on news stands. The modest little book, bound in green board with a linen back and a sticker on the spine to give the title, sold out in two months and brought the author a profit of $230. By a happy accident, one of the copies was purchased by the English publisher John Lane, who was on a visit to Canada, and he offered to bring it out under the imprint of The Bodley Head, his own distinguished and very successful firm. Thus Leacock's career as a humorist of world-reputation was launched.

Some of Leacock's favourite themes appear in this first book. "My Financial Career" is a brilliant sketch of a naive young man, baffled by a bank and at last forced into an assumption of a worldliness he cannot support. "The Awful Fate of Melpomenus Jones" tells of a curate who could not summon up the resolution to say that he must leave when making a pastoral call, and who died at last of social mortification in the home of his hosts. "Telling His Faults" gives us a hint of Leacock's characteristic attitude toward women: he seems never to have trusted them, and in the whole body of his work we rarely meet one who is completely likeable. "Lord Oxhead's Secret" is an example of his fascination with parody and of his hit-or-miss way of setting about it. "Number Fifty-Six" is uncharacteristic; in it Leacock is trying to imitate some model who has taken his fancy – might it have been O. Henry? – and the result is an ingenious but rather wooden piece of work, wrought with a care uncommon and unsuitable to the writer. "Self-Made Men" prefigures several descriptions that were to follow, through the years, of men of wealth anxious to impress their hearers with accounts of their early struggles.

There is some of Leacock's purest gold in this first book. "Boarding-House Geometry" is a brilliant distillation of the dregs of those fourteen Toronto boarding-houses in which he had lived during his college days and a transmutation of the bitter essence into unexpected splendour. "The Conjuror's Revenge" will always find its way to the heart of anyone who has had to brave the ignominy of a jackass's public criticism. "Society Chit-Chat," particularly that portion of it headed "Diner de Fameel at the Boarding House de McFiggin," is an early example of the undeluded eye with which Leacock examined much of social life. The book ends with "A, B, and C," which is certainly one of his finest flights of fantasy and

Feast of Stephen

of the quality of brilliant nonsense which made some critics liken him to Lewis Carroll.

Encouraged by his success (and a new kind of success at the age of forty must be encouraging indeed), Leacock wrote a more coherent piece of work. *Nonsense Novels,* published in 1911, is a series of ten parodies of popular forms of literature. As parodies they have nothing of the exactitude and penetration of the work of masters in this difficult genre; compare Leacock's efforts with Max Beerbohm's *A Christmas Garland* to discover where the work of the great parodist excels. Leacock had neither the fineness of ear nor the piercing literary perception that parody of a particular writer demands. Yet these ten pieces have characteristics often lacking in parody of a finer grain; they are only slightly touched by malice, they are vividly alive in themselves (and thus enjoyable without reference to known originals), and they are extremely funny.

They parody genres of novels, rather than particular writers, yet we find something both of Sherlock Holmes and Sexton Blake in the Great Detective of "Maddened By Mystery." "'Q' A Psychic Pstory of the Psupernatural" suggests something of Algernon Blackwood and perhaps also of Arthur Machen, whose stories made some flesh creep but left other flesh quiescent. "Guido the Gimlet of Ghent" suggests Maurice Hewlett and his school, especially Charles Major. "Gertrude The Governess" and "A Hero in Homespun" are parodies each of which might own a score of originals; the very names suggest genres within genres. But "Sorrows of a Super Soul: or, The Memoirs of Marie Mushenough," is pretty plainly aimed at Marie Bashkirtsev, whose journals and letters had an astonishing vogue among fanciers of the Slavic Soul. "Hannah of the Highlands" strongly suggests the Kailyard School novels of Ian Maclaren (pseudonym of John Watson) and S. R. Crockett. Probably the most quoted and misquoted invention of Leacock's is Lord Ronald, in "Gertrude the Governess," who "flung himself upon his horse and rode madly off in all directions," but I have a fondness for the feuding fathers in "Hannah":

Shamus McShamus, an embittered Calvinist, half-crazed perhaps with liquor, had maintained that damnation could be achieved only by faith. Whimper McWhinus had held that damnation could be achieved also by good works.

"Soaked in Seaweed" gets at the diseased marrow of many a tale of the sea; undoubtedly Frank T. Bullen is one of its targets. "Caroline's Christmas" seems to owe much to the stage; indeed, a part of the plot goes back to Lillo's *Fatal Curiosity*, but the whole suggests Denman Thompson's *The Old Homestead*. "The Man in Asbestos" sounds like H. G. Wells; the tone of the prose is not right, but the extravagant faith in the future is unmistakable. However, none of these ten pieces is tied to a single original; Leacock was both too exuberant and too impatient to work out a sharply defined parody of another man's style. The great parodist's palate is keen, his ear is delicately attuned to nuance, and there is about his work a feline, treacherous quality. None of these things could ever be said of Leacock; the slap-stick for him every time – never the rapier. Nor has he much care for exactitude, or he would not attribute Jeremy Taylor's *Holy Living and Holy Dying* to Bunyan, as he does in "Caroline's Christmas," and allow the error to run through all subsequent editions. Leacock simply does not give a damn about things for which scholars, and great parodists, give whole Infernos of damns.

As a general observation, there is usually much to be learned from a chronological study of an author's work, and Leacock is a case in point. His next production, in 1912, was *Sunshine Sketches of a Little Town*, and if it may not be called a novel, it has a strong appearance of being the work of a man who will write a novel very soon. The twelve chapters have a single setting and a group of characters who are developed by means of description from a variety of viewpoints. Although the term "sketches" suggests looseness of form, we find that the book must be read straight through, if we are to comprehend it fully; chapters may be extracted, as they have been by more than one anthologist, but no chapter is wholly self-contained. Read it as a novel, and all the characters fall into a coherent pattern, and the strong sense of the Little Town itself becomes so palpable that we know the Little Town to be the hero, the theme to which all else is contributory.

Descriptions of small-town life have become commonplace, especially in the literature of this continent. In Leacock's day they tended, with a handful of notable exceptions, to look on the sunny side of village and rural life and to accept the widely-held view that small-town people were kindlier, less corrupt, and more chaste than dwellers in great cities. Since then, of course, a school has arisen which portrays small towns, very profitably, as microcosms of Sodom and Gomorrah in which everybody but a handful of just men and women are deep in corruption, especially of the sexual order. Leacock tried very hard to keep his Sunshine Sketches sunny.

He succeeds, but only because he takes a determinedly god-like view of his community. Josh Smith, the hotel-keeper, is plainly the ablest man in Mariposa. He cannot read, though he can write his name, and he seems to have started his career as a cook in a logging-camp. But he has the Napoleonic touch. He disregards the law by keeping his saloon open after hours, and when the licensing authorities become troublesome, he exerts himself and spends a great deal of money to make his hotel so attractive that his fellow-citizens cannot bear to be without it and petition the licensing authorities to overlook his fault. As soon as this can be achieved, Josh cuts his expenses; the "caff" and the Rats' Cooler lose their gloss. (Josh never establishes the "Girl Room" that he has seen in big-city hotels, and this is a fine touch; a "Girl Room" would never do in Mariposa.) When the big mining boom comes north of the village everybody invests, but only Josh knows what will make money. When the *Mariposa Belle* sinks in Lake Wissanotti, Josh is the man who knows how to get her off a sandbank. When the Anglican Church gets into deeper water than the *Mariposa Belle* ever sailed, it is Josh who resolves its problems by burning it down and, as self-elected head of the fire brigade, knows how to keep the fire from spreading to the rest of the wooden town. And at last Josh gets himself elected to Parliament because he is willing to put money rather than principle into the campaign. We are not told so, but we can imagine that Josh went to Ottaway with one determination – to protect the interests of his constituents in every respect in which they happened to coincide with his own. Josh is indeed a finely executed portrait of a type of local tycoon and politician very important in Canadian politics so long as Canada remained a predominantly rural country, and by no means yet extinct. He is also a creature for whom Leacock never lost his admiration – the Man of Horse Sense, the leader who will always rise above the commonalty, whatever his want of education or principle.

When reading this book we should not miss the slight but convincing portrait of Josh's clerk, Billy, who does all the leg-work and spreads the word of the leader among the ranks. Billy is shadowy, because Billies always are so, but anybody with any experience of politics knows that every Josh has his Billy and could not work without him.

After Josh, the most carefully realized character is that of the Reverend Rupert Drone, the rural dean who has been

rector of the Anglican Church for forty years. He is as innocent and ineffectual as Josh Smith is worldly-wise and energetic. Yet there burns in him, as it does in the bosom of so
many priests, the ambition to build, to set up a bigger church,
and with the aid of his congregation, he does it. The Dean is
wholly unable to keep his accounts straight, probably because his education concentrated chiefly on classics; indeed,
though he cannot positively be said to read Greek, he is
frequently to be seen sleeping with a volume of Theocritus
on his knee. His real enthusiasm is for the minor achievements of engineering; he makes toys for children, and makes
them with skill. His world seems peaceful – though he thinks
he is run off his feet with church concerns – until he hears a
parishioner say that the church would be better off if that old
mugwump were out of the pulpit. This remark preys on him
until he determines to resign his charge. His decision coin-
cides with Josh Smith's recognition of the fact that the only
way to save the church from the Dean's mismanagement is to
burn it down and get its unrealistically large insurance value.
And so Josh saves the Dean, too, for although his wits are a
little astray, he is able to remain in his charge, assisted by a
curate.

Exaggerated? Only enough to be in key with the prevailing
harmony of the book; not so much as to be absurd, for who
does not know of good, ineffectual men who have lingered in
a backwater until, to their dismay, the backwater becomes
troubled water. The Dean exemplifies a feeling of Leacock's
that seems to have had the strength of a conviction, that the
clergy, and organized religion itself, were not forces in any
community, great or small, and that the advances of mankind
were brought about by economic and political, rather than by
spiritual agencies. For him the clergy, and one supposes
Christianity as well, had not much to do with life.

Jefferson Thorpe, the barber of Mariposa, is given a less
extended, but a sufficient, examination. Like all the Mariposa
people, Jeff is at once a type and an individual. When the
mining boom north of the little town awakens its cupidity,
he becomes an investor and, because of his stubbornness,
rather than through any acuity, he is a lucky one. He gets
forty thousand dollars – a fortune to a man who charges five
cents for a shave. But Jeff also acquires a conviction that
he is a shrewd fellow, although he knows nothing of invest-
ment except what he reads in the city papers. He is deferred
to by his customers as a man of uncommon insight. But he
puts his fortune in Cuban land speculation and loses it, and

thus goes right on shaving for five cents a shave, and his wife continues to supply eggs to Josh Smith's "caff." This too is a familiar story. Indeed, the writer of this study can recall himself as a little boy sitting on the board across the arms of a barber's chair, getting a haircut while the barber (a man who had probably never possessed $250 all at one time in his life) blew the scent of Wrigley's Spearmint Gum into his ear as he whispered: "If I had a cool fifty thou right this minute, I'd crack 'er all into Hollinger."

The fourth theme given extended treatment in the book is the romance of Peter Pupkin, the bank clerk, and Zena Pepperleigh, daughter of the district judge of Missinaba County. Here Leacock is less sure of his ground, and his tone moves farther from comedy into the realm of farce. He never had a completely assured hand when he wrote of love, which he seems to have linked with religion as one of those amiable delusions to which clouded or inferior intellects are subject. But who knows? In Mariposa it may have been so; rural Ontario has never had the name of being one of Aphrodite's favourite domains. Marriage – yes, Leacock can speak well of marriage. The link between the Judge and Martha Pepperleigh easily stands the strain of the Judge's fiery temper. Dean Drone's tender memories of his wife are first among the elements in his character that raise him above the level of the comic parson of platitudinous farce. But love –? We are never persuaded that Peter and Zena find anything of more than superficial value in one another. Zena is pretty: Peter proves to be the son of a rich man. The Judge and Peter's father have known each other in earlier days. And this is deemed enough. If there is to be anything of greater worth, it will presumably come after marriage and the baby. Leacock, like so many writers who aspire to popularity, declares himself to be fond of youth, but he writes most warmly of it when youth is disposed in well-ordered ranks in the university lecture room, taking notes.

This is not to say that Leacock knew nothing of tenderness. Jeff Thorpe, who refers to his wife simply as "the woman," is delighted with his gains because they will further the histrionic ambitions of his daughter Myra. Judge Pepperleigh is presented to us as something more than a legal bully because of his unwillingness to see that his son Neil is worthless, and the few sentences in which his grief at Neil's death in the South African war is described are among the most powerful in the book. Certainly Leacock knew tenderness; perhaps he knew too much of it and feared to allow himself to write of it.

But a man who seeks to be a novelist must conquer such fears and discipline his emotions to serve his artistic needs. The fact that Leacock never wrote of love except in a jocular and scoffing spirit tells us much about him. That he could love, we know; that he could not write about love, except as a joke, suggests that he never completely trusted his talent to express his deepest feelings.

Certainly *Sunshine Sketches* looks like a move toward writing novels, as Leacock's heroes and exemplars, Dickens and Mark Twain, had done. The godlike view, the assumption by the writer of a power to judge his characters, certainly leads toward the composition of novels of a particular kind. If he had persisted, Leacock might have written another kind of novel – the kind in which characters are described from the inside, instead of being examined from the outside; *David Copperfield* and *Huckleberry Finn* are such novels, known to him and admired by him. But something happened that seems to have warned Leacock away from this sort of work. The Little Town sharply resented the way in which it had been examined; the author's idea of sunshine seemed to it much more like an inquisitor's spotlight. Only a man of Leacock's remarkable self-confidence and lack of sensitivity toward other people could have thought that it would be otherwise. Strip the book of its humour, and what have we? A community in which the acknowledged leaders are windbags and self-serving clowns, and where the real leader is an illiterate saloon-keeper; a community that sees financial acuity in a lucky little barber who makes a one-in-a-thousand killing in the stock-market; a community that will not support a church, but will swindle an insurance company with a fraudulent fire; a community in which an election is shamelessly rigged; to say nothing of a community where a schoolteacher who takes an occasional glass of beer is "the one who drinks"(and thus an unfit person to receive a raise in pay), where the captain of the lake-boat cannot keep it off a shoal, and where a chance encounter betwen a nightwatchman and a bank clerk becomes a tale of heroism. We may all know of towns where some of these things or others of the same kind are true, but which of us would boast of being the original of Dean Drone, Judge Pepperleigh, or John Henry Bagshaw? The Little Town was very angry, and some of its citizens were still angry after Leacock died. It was later that he became a tourist attraction and the occasion of an annual award and banquet to which only his own pen could do proper satiric justice.

18   *Feast of Stephen*

During the greater part of his career Leacock reiterated, at intervals, his conviction that true humour springs from kindliness and gives no pain. He must have known, in his heart of hearts, that humour is a razor, and even in the most skilled hand it sometimes cuts. The humorist, if we take the word seriously, is akin to the writer of tragedy in his ability to see beneath the surface of life and to see what other men do not see. Of both the comic and the tragic writer people of commonplace outlook say the same thing – that he has exaggerated. Many artists, both in comedy and tragedy, are so naïve as to expect that humanity will be grateful to them for showing how absurd, or how desperate, human life can be. Leacock showed such naïveté toward Orillia and seems to have been both astonished and warned by the fury and hurt feelings he provoked. He never struck so truly again. He wanted to be liked, and that is a serious weakness in an artist of any kind. He gained his desire, for he was greatly liked – even loved, as time wore on. But his artistry was nipped by an early frost that succeeded the sunshine of the Little Town.

Throughout his life Leacock showed a strange innocence, a lack of self-knowledge, and a corresponding insensitivity toward others. He had no desire to hurt anybody's feelings, but he lacked insight into other people's feelings. The originals of some of the characters in *Sunshine Sketches* were indignant, others were wounded. In an article he wrote for the *Orillia Packet and Times* (March 12, 1957), Dr. C. H. Hale identifies several of those who were originals of characters in the book, and says that –

It was in deference to his mother that in the book version of *Sunshine Sketches,* Stephen disclaimed "any intention of doing anything so ridiculous as writing about a real place and real people" and in particular declared that "the Rev. Mr. Drone is not one person but about eight or ten." Mrs. Leacock had reproached her gifted son for lampooning her rector, Canon Greene, easily the most beloved man who ever lived in Orillia, whose tolerant kindliness was demonstrated by the fact that he never resented the rather cruel exploitation of his idiosyncracies.

Dr. Hale says that in its original version, which appeared serially in the Montreal *Star,* the names were even less disguised than in the book: Rapley and McCosh, who first appeared as Popley and McGraw, became Mullins and Pepperleigh. But Jeff Shortt, the Orillia barber, was still clearly Jefferson Thorpe, just as Bingham the undertaker was Golgotha Gingham. Josh Smith was – quite simply – still Josh Smith. It was for his caricature of Canon R. W. E. Greene that Leacock's mother, as Dr. Hale says, "gave Stephen Hail Columbia!"

It cannot have been the hurt feelings caused by *Sunshine Sketches* that brought about the scrappy form and shallow tone of *Behind the Beyond,* which succeeded it in 1913. Leacock wrote and published so much that one book was in the process of writing while its predecessor was still at the publisher's. There is nothing in this new volume that suggests the earlier and richer vein. The title-piece is a satire on the "problem plays" of the period; Leacock attacks them with his broad-axe but he has not been as concise here as he was in *Nonsense Novels.* He could touch off "Gertrude the Governess" in twenty pages; "Behind the Beyond" trudges on for forty, and it is too much for anything he has to say. He is happier in the group of five "Familiar Incidents" that follow it. But "Parisian Pastimes" is in his Mark Twain manner; here we have the Innocent Abroad comparing Paris with things back home. What Mark Twain did well in 1869 Leacock does poorly in 1913. We simply do not believe in him. Mark Twain was a genuine Innocent – ill-educated, and confined by a frontier outlook; Leacock is highly educated and has seen much of the world. Spurious naïveté is even more depressing than spurious sophistication. In the last piece in this book, "Homer and Humbug," he makes one of his many assaults on the classics, and the theme brings out much of what is best in his wit. It also reveals one of his convictions that time has not treated kindly – his faith in progress as a simple effect of the passing of time. "The classics are only primitive literature. They belong in the same class as primitive machinery and primitive music and primitive medicine," he says. We now see virtue in what is primitive, and we do not think of the passing of time as inevitably bringing improvement. In his faith in progress Leacock was very much a Victorian – a surprisingly simple Victorian.

His simplicity was by no means a constant quality, however. He followed the poor stuff of *Behind the Beyond* with *Arcadian Adventures with the Idle Rich* in 1914. In a lecture delivered at Harvard in 1968, Professor Claude Bissell described this as "his finest book," and supports this judgement with some illuminating comment on Leacock's political philosophy, and in particular Leacock's debt to Thorstein Veblen, with whom Leacock had studied during his Chicago years. Viewed thus, the book is unquestionably a fine one;

Leacock's distrust of the accumulation and manipulation of wealth in the hands of a plutocracy was an understandable outcome of his theories as an economist, and in describing the book as "almost a fictional companion piece to *The Theory of the Leisure Class*" Professor Bissell puts it in an interesting light. But the book would never have been written if economic theory were its mainspring; it is Leacock's distaste for the plutocrats themselves that gives it bite, and this distaste is at least as much the outcome of his own nurture in a Victorian gentlemanly tradition, supported by a classical education. Leacock dislikes plutocrats because they tend to be vulgarians, and he hits them as he never hit the simple folk of Mariposa. In consequence, although the book has more energy than *Sunshine Sketches*, it has less depth and is less impressive as a work of art.

Is it unduly fanciful to see the effect of a classical background in the names he gives some of his plutocratic characters? Lucullus, Asmodeus, and Gildas are surely the last names a self-made man would be likely to be given at the font. And the professors who appear fleetingly in the book are unworldly men, to whom money means nothing, and "accurate knowledge" everything; they may lack self-preservative qualities, but at least they are not taken in by the supposed financial wizardry of Tomlinson of Tomlinson's Creek, who is a Jefferson Thorpe of a larger growth. The typical plutocrat's combination of greed and gullibility is one of the things that sticks in Leacock's throat and rouses his hatred.

Indeed, it seems at times as if he were writing of Roman society during its decline. So many elements are the same: over-eating and drinking at luxurious meals, vulgar patronage of trivial artists and artificers, the toadying of priests and learned men to their intellectual inferiors, the abuse of innocence (for so we may interpret the spoliation of Mr. Peter Spillikins by Mrs. Everleigh and her lover), and above all by the prevalent superstition and trifling with sacred things.

Declining Rome went whoring after strange gods who came (as the strangest gods always do) from the East. So also does Mrs. Rasselyer-Brown whore after Mr. Yahi-Bahi, the celebrated Oriental mystic. How Leacock escaped suit by some agency of the Bahai faith is a mystery, for this certainly seems to be a scarcely veiled reference to the religion founded by Baha Ullah, and spread by his son, Sir Abdul Bahai (1844-1921), until it came to rest at Wilmette, Illinois. Mr. Yahi-Bahi instructs Mrs. Rasselyer-Brown and her selected friends on the principles of Boohooism, assisted by his disciple, Mr. Ram Spudd; they progress rapidly through Swaraj (Denial of Self) toward Stoj (Negation of Thought) until a few attain to Bahee, or the Higher Indifference; they are even granted a vision of Buddha, which is in reality Mr. Rasselyer-Brown in his dressing-gown, seeking a late drink at the sideboard. At last Mr. Yahi-Bahi and Mr. Ram Spudd are arrested by the chauffeur, who is a disguised policeman, just as they are about to make off with the jewels and furs of the worshippers.

The satire is crude, but a vigorous anger sustains it. Leacock detests idle, shallow women, and he detests crooks. But we also receive a strong impression that he detests mysticism, too. He never jeered at religion, though he never said anything to support any form of belief; stoicism seems to have been his refuge in trouble. But he hated triviality about great matters.

There are perhaps no pages in all of Leacock so bitter or so carefully controlled from the standpoint of literary artistry as the two chapters in this book called "The Rival Churches of St. Asaph and St. Osoph" and "The Ministrations of the Reverend Uttermust Dumfarthing." Briefly, St. Asaph's is in the ascendant when he begins their history, and it prospers under the care of a dashing, fashionable, and personable young Episcopal priest, the Reverend Edward Fareforth Furlong; meanwhile St. Osoph's, a Presbyterian church, was being emptied by its minister, the Reverend Doctor McTeague, who believed in sin and spent his time trying to reconcile Hegel and St. Paul. But when at last Dr. McTeague has an accident and is replaced by the exuberant, fire-breathing prophet of eternal damnation, the Reverend Uttermust Dumfarthing, he is so dynamic, so deliciously alarming that he draws away Furlong's fashionable congregation.

What is to be done? Plutoria Avenue knows, for it is the preserve of the most acute financial minds in both congregations. A merger is the only answer to the problem. Throw the churches together! The result? "Rivalry, competition, and controversies over points of dogma have become unknown on Plutoria Avenue. The parishioners of the two churches may now attend either of them just as they like. As the trustees are fond of explaining, it doesn't make the slightest difference." Leacock detests this sort of flabbiness, where principle runs a bad second to financial or administrative expediency, in every realm of life, and his disgust that it should invade religion is apparent. He was a man of great goodwill, but there was nothing oecumenical about him.

This very angry book, like *Sunshine Sketches,* suggests that its author could have written novels if he had been willing to submit himself to the discipline of a plot and characters who are drawn at length. But it is foolish to regret that Leacock did not compel himself to write novels; his sense of character is strong, but his plots are at most those of a writer of short stories. He was wise not to drive himself to work for which he was unfitted by temperament, for there was in him nothing of the patient weaver of a long story. He seems to have worked in bursts of inspiration, though his habits of work were regular. In matters of narrative he was a sprinter, not a miler. But in *Arcadian Adventures* and *Sunshine Sketches,* he composed two books which, without being novels, have unity, and leave a single strong impression on the reader.

In 1915 his book, now becoming an annual affair, was *Moonbeams from the Larger Lunacy.* In the Preface, the author explains his method of producing a book:

> The prudent husbandman, after having taken from his field all the straw that is there, rakes it over with a wooden rake and gets as much again. The wise child, after the lemonade jug is empty, takes the lemons from the bottom of it and squeezes them into a still larger brew. So does the sagacious author, after having sold his material to the magazines and been paid for it, clap it into book-covers and give it another squeeze. . . .

He then acknowledges permission from *Vanity Fair, The American Magazine, The Popular Magazine, Life, Puck, The Century,* and *Methuen's Annual* to re-publish. These were not the only magazines to which Leacock contributed in his time; he wrote for virtually all the popular magazines that printed humour, and for many university publications that were not, strictly speaking, commercial ventures, for he was generous in this respect. In attempting to form a just estimate of Leacock's work we must remember that he wrote in an era when magazines were many and all but the most high-brow welcomed short, funny pieces. It was these that he brought together for many of his annual books.

This throws light on some of his subject matter; it was timely then, and we need not be surprised, or aggrieved against the author, if it is timely no more. "Spoof: A Thousand Guinea Novel" is parody of a genre – the prize novel from a contest supported by a magazine or publishing house – which has changed out of all recognition; "Ram Spudd The New World Singer" is about the eternal fashionable poet, but the fashion has changed. "Truthful Oratory" and "Who Is Also Who" would have been welcome nonsense if we had found them in the pages of the magazines in which they once appeared; to read them solemnly now, having drawn up all the heavy artillery of the past sixty years of criticism, is to deal unfairly. They were lilies of a day, and their day is long past. *Moonbeams* is not a book we can take up now with the certainty of pleasure. Much of the work of many humorists belongs in the same category, as those who have chewed through collected volumes of Robert Benchley, James Thurber, or S. J. Perelman can testify. It was written to be taken in small doses, and when it is read by the volume it produces the ennui of an interminably extended night-club act. Only schoolboys and tired businessmen have any gusto for so much remorseless fun. But we must bear in mind that in their time, and taken singly, these slight pieces were superior work.

It is in *Moonbeams* that we find Leacock's first references to the Great War of 1914-18. They are tentative, for he was writing chiefly for American magazines, and though the United States was interested, it was not yet irrevocably involved. But Leacock was involved, and sometimes we sense his concern beneath his controlled tone.

The following year brought another book of the same order, but in *Further Foolishness* there is a section of eighty-eight pages called "Peace, War and Politics" that is out of keeping with the fashionably funny tone of the rest of the book, and even has five illustrations, very poor in themselves, by M. Blood, though the frontispiece is by A. H. Fish, the accomplished illustrator usually assigned to Leacock by John Lane. The five chapters in this section are angry and not very amusing; the last of them, "The White House from Without Within," is in the form of a diary kept by Woodrow Wilson and it suggests the twistings and squirmings of a man determined to ignore a world peril. Leacock was losing his temper – and like steel that has lost its temper, he hacks when he means to cut.

It was 1916 also which saw the appearance of a collection of more serious writing, called *Essays and Literary Studies*, containing some of Leacock's most characteristic work. He has not striven to be funny in these; the humour has arisen naturally and it is inextricable from the fabric of the thought, instead of being a matter of formula or contrivance. "The Apology of a Professor" is still fully relevant to the essentials of higher education; it is an appeal for the mind full of thought, as opposed to the bellyful of fact, for a university where students really want to learn and professors really have something to teach. "Literature and Education in America" is still a fine consideration of the intelligence of this continent, and of graduate education. "American Humour" is a highly professional critical study, better than much on this theme that was to follow. "The Lot of the Schoolmaster" approaches fearlessly a topic now almost as dangerous as anti-Semitism or the Advancement of Coloured Peoples – that is, the intellectual and moral stultification of a large number of people who take on the work of instructing the young. Leacock always considered school-teaching a dangerous job for anybody, and an impossible one for men of first-rate abilities, if they did not also happen to be educational geniuses.

As this volume exhibits his strength, it also shows one of his weaknesses. "The Amazing Genius of O. Henry" is an essay of unstinting praise of a man whose work has not stood the test of time. We do not now submit to the surprise endings and coincidences of O. Henry as did his contemporaries, but we are even more impatient of his sentimentality. Of course, every age has its favoured brand of sentimentality, and our own is no exception; but we cannot now swallow the combination of toughness and sweetness, served up with a smart-alec grin and a boozy tear, which was O. Henry's stock-in-trade. Leacock may well have been dazzled by O. Henry's success, but we are astonished that he should have referred to this formula-writer as "one of the great masters of modern literature," whose full stature is still to be discovered. Perhaps what astonishes us most is that Leacock appears to consider O. Henry a writer greatly superior to himself. Leacock was a man of inferior literary taste and a capricious and variable critic; of his own real worth he seems to have had no idea; as a writer he has twenty strings to his bow for O. Henry's one – thrilling and plangent though that single string appeared to be.

The book of gleanings for 1917 was *Frenzied Fiction*. The war colours it; "My Revelations as a Spy" is one of the parodies of a genre, and "Father Knickerbocker" is an attempt to flatter the war spirit of the United States which now seems painfully mechanical; Leacock had a heavy hand as a propagandist. But "The Errors of Santa Claus" is one of his best inventions, fit to stand with "My Financial Career," "Boarding-House Geometry," and "A, B, and C." We may linger also over "Back from the Land," a chapter of autobiography that is sometimes forgotten; it is Leacock's confession of how he tried to run his place at Old Brewery Bay on scientific, or business, or economic principles, and how Nature defeated him. It is in the vein of *Essays and Literary Studies*, and this, after the inspired humour of his finest comic work, is his best manner and the one he could always command.

The year 1919 brought the book which shows us Leacock at his worst, *The Hohenzollerns in America*. Beating the bones of the vanquished is poor fun, and if Leacock thought he had to do it, we may fittingly wish that he had brought his best gifts to the job. But this cheap jeering at the German Emperor, vulgar sneering at Ferdinand of Bulgaria, and sour detraction directed at the German Crown Prince, grates on us. Nevertheless, we may not dismiss it; he wrote it, and if we accept his sunshine, we must not shrink from a peep into the dank chill of his shade.

It is written in the form of fragments of a diary of an imaginary Princess Frederica of Hohenzollern, and it describes the immigration of the royal personages of the defeated Central Powers to the United States, where they look for jobs. The Emperor William is mad and his shrivelled arm debars him from physical labour, so he ends as a hawker of cheap badges and ribbons on the Bowery; he thinks they are royal decorations, and the Boweryites regard him as a "character" known as "Old Dutch," until he dies in a Pauper Hospital. Ferdinand of Bulgaria makes a fortune as a crooked garment manufacturer. The Crown Prince is apprehended as a sneak thief. The Princess marries a kindly iceman. What makes us cringe as we read this stuff is that Leacock has so plainly aimed it at minds greatly inferior to his own, to feed a nasty kind of patriotism and mean triumph. Even when we try to consider it as part of an hysterical post-war relief, it is still bad Leacock, and the other things in the book, including the satire on plutocrats who profited from the war but sent their chauffeurs to fight, are no better.

He recovers his strength in 1920; *Winsome Winnie and other New Nonsense Novels* is, in my opinion, better than *Nonsense Novels*; the touch is surer, the satire more skilled. "Buggam Grange: A Good Old Ghost Story" is one of Leacock's neatest parodies of a genre.

The apparent rise in spirits brings superior workmanship. The next book, *My Discovery of England*, published in 1922, is one of Leacock's finest. What he wrote from personal experience is always more consistent in level than his imagined humorous sketches, and in this volume "Oxford as I See It" and "We Have With Us Tonight" rank among the best work of his lifetime.

Although his own education was Canadian and American, Leacock had a natural affinity with the Oxford system – which appears to a casual glance to be no system at all. He liked the roominess of the Oxford approach, which provided in the same university a happy playtime for light-hearted and unintellectual young men, and a broad prospect of the world's humanistic knowledge (it was not at that time much good at science) for those who wanted to study. Oxford somehow managed to deposit a faint dust of learning on the former and persuaded the latter that learning, however deep, ought to be worn with modesty. The humanism of Oxford, he thought, contrasted very favourably with the efficiency of American universities, and he recognized that the Oxonian desipience concealed a great deal of slogging hard work, whereas the strenuosity of the American institutions could often leave them open to narrow specialization, formula criticism, and downright anti-intellectualism. Particularly, he admired the command of English style that Oxford could impress upon a young man whose American equivalent was impervious to such influence. The Oxford he visited was still resistent to co-education and he liked that, too, for in his opinion co-education had no value but its relative cheapness; he did not deny the right of women to education, but he could see no sense in educating them as if they were men. Such an attitude, heretical in his own day, is thought merely laughable now; it may be another century before we recognize that Leacock was right, and that a woman's intellect, at its best, is not the same as a man's, and that its differences make it fascinating but not inferior; the world needs both.

Is there anything in literature that explores the situation of the public speaker, paid or unpaid, so sensitively and poignantly as " 'We Have With Us Tonight' "? Public speaking, as Leacock knew as well as any man in the past century, is at its best a form of art and a special type of entertainment. He was a master of it as university lecturer and as platform performer. As a professor in a classroom he knew that, whatever the word "lecture" may imply etymologically and historically, the thing itself should be an experience not to be duplicated simply by reading the same words from a book; the professor worthy of the name establishes an intimacy of contact with his students that is in itself illuminating and inspiring. The good professor is himself an example of what learning makes of a man; if he is a dullard, learning must be dull; if he is half-literate, learning is diminished; if he is torpid with boredom and poisoned with scholarly scruple, learning appears as a disease. His job is not to utter ultimate and unchallengeable truth, but to make his students sufficiently interested to take on his subject themselves and confute him if he needs to be confuted. Without becoming a clown of the lecture-hall, a professor must make himself interesting.

Much more so the public speaker. Everybody who has had experience in this line knows how intractable the usual audience is, how reluctant to be wooed into a receptive whole. Yet he must woo, or he will never win, and if he does not win his speech has been a waste of time for himself and everybody else. But how rarely does he speak in an atmosphere that is not positively hostile to him! After luncheon or dinner, people are heavy with food and drink, and all too often several speakers have said what they call "a few words" before him. An evening lecture is usually given in a room where the speaker is in a bad light, and his audience, unless he is lucky enough to have filled the hall, spread among many seats. Leacock describes his sensations on being asked to give a humorous talk from the pulpit of a church!

The greatest hazard, as Leacock saw it, was the chairman, whose introduction so often put the lecturer to the bad for the first ten minutes of his speech. We can only conclude that chairmen never read, or else in the time since he wrote about them – now almost fifty years ago – they would have mended their ways. But they have not, as every speaker knows.

Leacock's own platform manner is sometimes said to have been based on that of Mark Twain, but this is certainly not true; just as he could not parody another writer with the accuracy of the master of parody, I think it unlikely that he could, or would, imitate any other man's platform manner. He seems never to have heard Mark Twain, who died in 1910. Insofar as Mark Twain was a master at planting a joke, delaying a climax, and leading from a good joke to an even better one, Leacock was like him; but these are the arts of a special sort of rhetorician, not the inventions of a single person. When Leacock appeared on the platform, in his beautiful but rumpled dress clothes, with his white tie untied because he never mastered the intricacies of the bow knot, with his thick grey hair rumpled but not frowzy, and his whole face beaming but not grinning, he was like nobody in the world but Stephen Leacock. Mark Twain's voice was a Southern drawl and not particularly resonant; Leacock's was deep and full, and his pronunciations were those of a man of cultivation. Mark Twain was, in his platform appearances, what is called a dry wit: Leacock had nothing dry about him

– he was a wet wit, and on a few recorded occasions so wet that he gave offence to temperance advocates among his hearers. Furthermore, Leacock laughed at his own jokes, which is regarded as technically dangerous for a humorist; only a master of assured originality could chance it. Leacock was not an imitator or a revived Mark Twain; his comic genius was at its highest pitch when it was bodied forth by his unique platform personality.

Not all of Leacock's chairmen were inept. His first lecture in London was introduced by Sir Owen Seaman, at that time editor of *Punch*; his speech, reprinted in *My Discovery*, is a model of what an introduction should be. It contains some perceptive comment on Leacock's special position as a Canadian, with one foot in Britain and the other in North America, so that his humour is British by heredity, but American by association, and "the truth is that his humour contains all that is best in the humour of both hemispheres."

Beyond this point, which brings Leacock to his fifty-third year, it seems needless to continue consideration and criticism of his writing on a chronological plan; his strengths and his weaknesses have all been demonstrated. He produced, single-handed or in collaboration, nearly sixty books, not counting pamphlets. We have looked at fourteen of them, and will look at others, but a consideration of all his work is neither possible nor desirable in such a study as this. I do not consider myself a proper person to write of either his historical books or the works on economics and political theory. Of these latter I am told by people able to judge that the history is readable but unoriginal, that the political theory is first-rate in a realm where opinion frequently changes, and that the economics is not highly regarded; indeed one able economist tells me that in this area Leacock "wrote some damn fool things."

This is not to say that he was not capable of teaching the elements of economics to undergraduates; it is agreed that he was a great teacher. But in this realm he was not an original thinker, though he sometimes tried to be one. He was, indeed, the victim of a Scottish peculiarity of McGill University, which linked economics and political theory in an old-fashioned way that has long been abandoned. Of his economics, therefore, let an economist judge. It is possible that professional criticism may be particularly severe on a man who so far offended against professionalism as to make his chief impact in another field – and humour at that.

Of his criticism, however, we may appropriately judge here. Leacock was not a literary critic in any effective sense except as a parodist of genres; he could spot the falsity, the convention, and the absurdity in popular books and mock them hilariously. This is in itself a great gift, but it is not criticism in the ordinary sense. Even in this realm he was too much an impressionist, too slapdash in manner, to give us the faint heart of any school of bad writing as Beerbohm, for instance, gives us the essential absurdity of a whole school of verse drama in *Savonarola Brown*. At his best Leacock makes us laugh, but tells us nothing about what we are laughing at, as the great parodist does. At his worst he succumbs to a kind of aggressive lowbrowism – in his day it was sometimes called the Mucker Pose – and we meet with a lot of this in a book of 1923, *Over the Footlights*. Those of us who have seen college productions of Greek tragedy will sense the truth of *Oroastus*, but when he turns to Ibsen he obviously does not know enough about Ibsen to be able to do more than jeer. He is even worse in his tiltings at Russian drama; the reader has the uncomfortable sensation that Leacock has heard about Russian drama but has certainly not seen or read much of it. The fine parodist must know his theme, must have qualities that might enable him to write about it seriously and – here is where Beerbohm scores so convincingly – must love it in its best manifestations. Leacock's subtlety, though not inconsiderable, did not lie in this direction.

Nor is he much better when he attempts serious criticism, as in *Charles Dickens: His Life and Work*, which appeared in 1933. In 1932 he had produced a good, modest study of Mark Twain, and doubtless its success encouraged him to try a more ambitious project. The Mark Twain book has value insofar as it is the opinion of one great humorist on another for whom he felt an affinity, but as Ralph L. Curry says in his biography of Leacock, it relies too heavily on the conclusions of Van Wyck Brooks' *The Ordeal of Mark Twain*. Leacock protested, as most humorists do, against the notion that writers of humorous books themselves live in an unvaried condition of euphoria; Mark Twain did not do so, and he certainly did not do so himself. What he produced was an affectionate, amusing short study in which there are some valuable insights. He seems to have understood very well that his work on Dickens was a more demanding project, but he gives no evidence of scholarly preparation, even to the extent of a careful re-reading of Dickens' works. Its errors extend even to the names of important characters, and there is a clumsiness of style which is not like Leacock at his best. We could overlook these blemishes if his ideas about Dickens were other than conventional, but it is clear that the Dickens Leacock admired was the ebullient young writer of the early period, the creator of Pickwick and Micawber. He delights in the flow of high spirits and the richness of comic invention. He deplores the melodrama of the plots, for he has not troubled to discover what melodrama is, or how it relates to Dickens' habit of mind, or the spirit of his age. Melodrama to him is simply old-fashioned absurdity, and Dickens ought to have seen through it; no notion of melodrama as a way of looking at life, and of giving it some of the compelling immediacy of a dream, seems to have occurred to him. Leacock simply wants Dickens to be funny, which is odd, considering the insight he extended toward Mark Twain; he dismisses the pathos of Little Nell and Paul Dombey, and the savagery of Bill Sikes, as artistic aberration. "Sorrow as a deliberate luxury is a doubtful pursuit, a dubious form of art," he says. We may ask, why? Why is it praise-worthy to be extravagant in mirth, but dubious to be extravagant in melancholy? I think this gives us an insight into the nature of Stephen Leacock, of whom it might be said, as it was of King Lear, "he hath ever but slenderly known himself." Any extreme of temperament is likely to be balanced by its opposite, and as Dickens was greatly comic, he was greatly pathetic. Did not Leacock sense this balancing of temperament in himself? We are told by those who knew him well that he had moods of deep melancholy and no trifling amount of savagery. Did Leacock dislike the melancholy in Dickens because he feared its echo in himself? Certainly his poor taste in poetry suggests that he shrank from works of art that invited a deeply serious response. He is an unsatisfactory critic of Dickens because he chooses to respond to only one of Dickens' moods.

His book enjoyed considerable success in its time, but we now find it out of key with the changed and enhanced reputation of Dickens that has emerged from the criticism of the past thirty-five years. Indeed, it was already out of key when it was written, for in 1932 Osbert Sitwell had published a brief but penetrating study of Dickens, which is still valuable. The reason is that Sitwell was really writing about Dickens, and Leacock, even in critical biography, could never venture far, or for long, beyond writing about Leacock.

His failure to accept Dickens as a whole, rather than as a great comic writer gone astray, dulls his perception of that later Dickens, which is now regarded as the author's greatest and most mature work. Leacock finds these novels "overplanned and uninspired." *Hard Times* he dismisses as a failure, of which "not a chapter or a passage in the book is part of Dickens' legacy to the world." How he had studied the book is suggested by his repeated references to Josiah Bounderby as "Bounderly"; one need not go all the way with Professor F. R. Leavis, in *The Great Tradition*, to reject this shallow judgement. And consider what he says about *Great Expectations:*

> The opening of the book – the hunted convict among the gravestones – the churchyard on the marshes by the sea – a picture taken from the view from Gad's Hill [sic] – is as wonderful an opening as only Dickens could make. But the story is throughout on a lower level than the greater books, the characters less convincing, the nullities more null, the plot more involved, the fun, what there is of it, apt to sound forced and mechanical. One looks in vain in its pages for world-famous characters. The ending, unexpectedly altered from tragedy to relief, at the suggestion of Bulwer Lytton, is as unconvincing as any end must be when fitted onto the beginning of something else.

The shrewd judgement in the final sentence comes oddly after the uncomprehending and insensitive comment that goes before. But that was Leacock – not bleakly bad, but fitful and impatient in criticism.

One other aspect of this book asks for consideration here. Leacock harps on Dickens' respectability. He never, says Leacock, felt the fetters of nineteenth century prudery as Mark Twain did. The sordid muddle of Dickens' parting from his wife is explored, but there is no mention of the name of Ellen Ternan. Yet Leacock acquainted himself with the terms of Dickens' will from John Forster's *The Life of Charles Dickens,* which is his primary source. Did he not observe that Dickens' first bequest in that will was "the sum of £1,000 free of legacy duty to Miss Ellen Lawless Ternan, of Houghton Place, Ampthill Square"? It is almost, as Edgar Johnson says in *Charles Dickens, His Tragedy and Triumph,* as if he desired to defy convention from the grave. Did it not occur to Leacock to wonder who Ellen Lawless Ternan was? Or, when he wrote, "Charles Dickens is not yet history, to be mauled about like Charles the Second or Charlemagne," was it the Victorian gentleman in him speaking? He was himself no bad keeper of personal secrets. As he grew older (and at this time he was sixty-four), some of his Victorian ideas became more noticeable.

They are given an effective airing in *Too Much College,*

which he published in 1939. Certainly it is one of the books of the later period of his life which we should not neglect. It is a protest against the over-valuation of a university degree, and against the dilution of the curriculum to ensure that large numbers of unscholarly people may achieve one. It is a lively work, written in Leacock's best combination of driving argument relieved with wit. Sometimes we may think that he is reversing earlier judgements, as when he recommends Latin – but "streamlined Latin" – as a valuable study for those who seek to write and speak English well. But he relaxes no jot of his hostility toward Greek, and says that "to my mind the wit of Aristophanes is about as funy as the jokes of a village cut-up. To name him in the class with people like Charles Dickens and Mark Twain and A. P. Herbert and Bob Benchley and myself is just nonsense." The tone of the book is of academic Toryism, but it is too full of hard-won experience and shrewd academic good sense to be brushed aside. Reading it, we think what so often Leacock made us think: "How good this is, how true! But if only he had been a little less self-indulgent, a little more strenuous in thought, a little less willing to mingle prejudice with insight, how much better it could have been!" This is not to criticize Leacock for not doing what lay outside his power; he could have written vastly better about educational and political problems if he had been stricter with himself and – it must be said – a little less patronizing, or contemptuous, toward his readers.

What fine things fall from his pen, almost, as it seems, by accident! In this volume the twelve hundred words he called "Reader's Junk" is a splendid exploration of the "accumulation in the reader's mind of a set of preconceptions, pictures and ready-made characters" with which he peoples and decorates the stories he reads. It puts forward a fascinating psychological observation, and says everything there is to be said about it, until some psychologist writes a profound study of it. This is the kind of thing Leacock could do, but seems always to have done inadvertently. He became impatient with a set task or a big theme, but his insights are often those of genius.

So too with *My Remarkable Uncle*, published in 1942. The sketch of E. P. Leacock that gives the book its name fixes forever the portrait of a particular type of English remittance man familiar in Canada until the outbreak of the First World War. Of polished manner, well-connected, personally delightful, E. P. Leacock could have charmed a bird from a tree – and probably did so, if he wanted to eat the bird. He was a dead-beat, a liar, and a crook, but for him, as with many others of his kind, these words lose much of their sting, because he was also a life-enhancing man; it was almost a pleasure, a source of distinction, to be swindled by such a person. Leacock has drawn him with honesty tempered by affection in one of the best of his short pieces.

In 1944 he published a book which any admirer of his would have wished unwritten, but which must be mentioned in a critical study because it gives us so many clues to Leacock's character and cast of mind. It is called, baldly, *How To Write;* an alternative, more accurate title might be, *How Leacock Read.* Obviously he read capriciously, rapidly, and inaccurately. There is no reason why he should have done otherwise; writers are not obliged to be good readers of other men's work. But when a writer sets out to tell novices how to write, he should not betray other men's work by inaccurate quotation, as Leacock does not only in this book, but in such productions as his otherwise good essay on W. S. Gilbert. Leacock appears to have had a tin ear; his sense of cadence or the fitness of words is negligible. He recalls A. A. Milne's

> You must never go down to the end of the town
> if you don't go down with me

as being

> You mustn't go down to the end of the town
> unless you go down with me

which limps badly. And he turns Dibdin's musical

> Here, a sheer hulk, lies poor Tom Bowling,
> The darling of our crew

into the stumbling

> Here's to the name of poor Tom Bo-owling
> The darling of the crew

Anyone with an ear better than a Member of Parliament — those artless mis-quoters — would have felt that those two "ofs" so close together must be wrong. But not Leacock; he seems to have had no understanding of music or of verse. In this book he quotes Tennyson's "Tears, idle tears, I know not what they mean," correctly in one chapter, but mauls the line into "Tears, idle tears, and yet I know not why," in another. The excuse that he wrote for the Belly and the Members will not serve here, for the Belly and the Members are fine judges of rhythm, rhyme, and all the bardic arts.

Did he care about accuracy? He was not under any compulsion to do so, but a man who offers aspiring writers so much advice inevitably seems to be patronizing them, and patronizing writers vastly greater than he, when he offers such a muddle as this. If he did not like poetry, why does he include two chapters on "How Not To Write Poetry"? His spleen is ungenerously vented on poets he dislikes. True, he seems to like Wordsworth and Herrick when they write about daffodils, but principally as an excuse to introduce a daffodil poem of his own, as it might be from the pen of "an up-to-date poet." Indeed, far too much of *How To Write* is used for lambasting authors who, in his opinion, do not know how to write. His taste is revealed as spotty and commonplace.

What he really likes is humour; however, he values it not as a quality of mind that may reveal itself in any sort of writing (a quality he possessed himself and evinced in some of his best expository work) but rather as deliberate comic invention. His favourites in this sort of creation are Mark Twain and Charles Dickens, and his taste led him to assert that Dickens was superior to Shakespeare, "a man – or a collection of men – of far lesser genius."

He offers two chapters on "How To Write Humour" in this unfortunate book. He establishes his topic thus: "Humour may be defined as the kindly contemplation of the incongruities of life and the artistic expression thereof." Leacock was very insistent on the necessity for humour to be kindly. Was it because he felt so strongly within him the impulse, known to many humorists and indulged by some of the best of them, to make fools wince? Was he still remembering the backlash of *Sunshine Sketches?* Certainly he twists his definition to fit Shakespeare's portrait of Falstaff, and he applies it liberally to the works of Dickens. He seems to have forgotten Pecksniff and Mrs. Gamp, who are certainly funny but not because of any kindliness in their depiction. And what did he make of Quilp, that splendid, cruel, comic grotesque? But in these chapters Leacock is not open to argument; he lays down the law, and like many who do that, he falls into platitude. "Writing originates in thinking . . . thinking is sincerity and interest in the world around you . . . writing comes from having something to say and trying hard to say it." Yes, Professor.

Happily his last book, published posthumously in 1946, contains some of his best writing. It is *The Boy I Left Behind Me;* it was compiled, at his wish, by his niece Barbara Nimmo and appeared with an affectionate preface by her. The first four chapters are all that we have of an autobiography he had been contemplating since 1942. The autobiographical style suited him perfectly. Indeed, he had been writing autobiography, in one disguise or another, all his life. Here he writes with the assurance of an old man and with a self-knowledge he has never before chosen to reveal. The manner is leisurely and digressive, but it evokes atmosphere with a sure artistry not previously achieved in any other extended work. The four chapters tell of his background and boyhood, of his life on the family farm, of his education, and of his experiences as a schoolmaster. Is it perverse to be glad he did not begin the book earlier and bring it to completion? So many autobiographies begin with fine descriptions of childhood and youth, only to drop as the years wear on into catalogues of names, and discreet accounts of a public career in which the innermost spirit of the writer seems to have been lost; Leacock's remains for us as a splendid beginning, from which we learn of many of the things that bore upon his best later writing. This is the key to Leacock, so far as a man who took such pains to conceal his deepest feelings ever gave us a key.

4

Like Mark Twain, Leacock was impatient with people who thought that a humorist must be a man who lived in a whirlwind of laughter, and thought life one vast joke. But – and again in this he is like Mark Twain and humorists generally – he never seems to have given any serious thought to what a humorist is, or where humour has its source. He wrote frequently about the technique of humour, but beyond advising his readers not to give away the point of a joke until the end, he has not much that is useful to say. What did he tell aspirants humour was? "The kindly contemplation of the incongruities of life and the artistic expression thereof." It is no impertinence toward his memory to say that he certainly knew better than that.

Let us look at the large body of his own work that he called humour. We can separate it into three categories. First comes a small group of pieces, most of them short, which we cannot imagine as having been written by anyone else; they are Stephen Leacock *per se*. Every careful reader of Leacock will have his own list, in which "Boarding-House Geometry," "A, B, and C," and "My Financial Career" will certainly have a place, along with selections amounting to perhaps twenty in all. I should like to make a claim on behalf of "Hoodoo McFiggin's Christmas" in *Literary Lapses,* which, he tells us, in "Christmas Shopping" (written thirty-two years afterward), was based on his own childhood disappointment. It is very funny and painfully sad. Professor Marshall McLuhan says that every humorist is a man with a grievance; Heinrich Heine said it in more compassionate fashion when he wrote, "Out of my great sorrows I make my little songs." A strong claim might be made for another Christmas piece, "The Errors of Santa Claus," which first appeared in *Puck* on December 2, 1916; it has something of the same pathos about it, more gently evoked. A few short pieces, *Sunshine Sketches* and *Arcadian Adventures* are the cream of Leacock.

When we have removed his best and most individual work,

we encounter a substantial body of writing which is not meant primarily to be funny, but to convey opinions; *My Discovery of England* (1922) is perhaps the best book in this realm, and *My Discovery of the West* (1937) is so perfunctory in tone that it does not deserve inclusion. But *Too Much College* – the first 164 pages of it – is a neglected book of this kind, and there are excellent individual essays in many of the later volumes. Leacock was a notable argumentative essayist. He is not a philosopher and he is not always logical, but he is persuasive and powerful. It is a particular pleasure to read him on education. This body of work certainly shows that Leacock was no mere funny-man; it reveals his humour as being in the grain of his intelligence; but by no means the dominating element of his spirit.

After these categories we must gather together a body of work which he wrote rapidly, carelessly, and often without any real purpose except to compose a "funny piece." Of this work it has already been said that it was for publication in magazines, and the point must be stressed if we are to see Leacock as part of the literary world of his period. It was a period much of which fell before the Depression that began in 1929, when the revolt against nineteenth-century thought and social custom that had followed the war of 1914-18 continued with unabated enthusiasm – a period of expansion, easy money, and good times. People liked to laugh, and there were several magazines that existed for no other purpose than to help them do so. Looking at these magazines now, we do not find them very funny, but unquestionably they are cheerful in intent. The people who read such magazines are now – they or their grandchildren – the public for funny television. It was to these magazines, for this public, that Leacock sold his "funny pieces" and amid the formula humour of their pages his contributions must have seemed distinguished. That they are so no longer is nobody's fault. There they are and we cannot ignore them; several of the yearly books, which appeared for the Christmas trade and were regularly bought by Leacock's addicted audience, consist of nothing else; we cannot pretend he did not write them, and they tell us a few things about him.

It is easy work for a critic to look backward over a writer's career and point out where he failed to be true to his gift, and in what ways he failed to live out such a career as the critic would think proper. But nobody lives according to a plan; everybody suffers ups and downs of energy and inventiveness, and everybody is influenced in his work by circumstances and traits of character that seem on the surface to have little to do with it. What were these traits in Leacock that made him write so much?

He seems to have admired industry for its own sake; he had the real Ontario farm boy's contempt for anybody who was shiftless. He despised stupidity, and idleness was one form of stupidity. He also liked money, because it brought respect, the kind of luxury he loved, and security; he might look down on the plutocrats who made a god of wealth, but he was proud of the fact that he, a McGill professor with a salary of about $6,000 yearly, had an income that for years ranged between forty and fifty thousand dollars, most of it earned with his pen. There was certainly nothing stupid about that. He had also a liking for speculation and sought to augment his fortune in the stock market. I cannot prove it, but I have been told by a friend of his who was prominent in the world of finance that Leacock invested on margin, and if that were so, the crash that preceded the Depression must have hit him very hard. It is certain that after that time he became extremely exacting about fees for his writing and for his lectures – so much so that it was a matter for comment if he lectured gratis in aid of a charitable cause. This would also explain his assumption of tasks that were beneath his dignity, such as the preparation of commissioned books which were essentially advertisements for commercial firms and the writing of an advertising pamphlet for a trust company. He needed money to support his ample style of living, and he may well have had the desire – by no means so uncommon as some people believe – to astonish the world with his fortune when he died. As it was, he left an estate, after probate, of $140,000, and as probated value is always well below the reality, he must have accumulated a substantial fortune after paying whatever his losses in the market may have been. If the sum named does not seem great to my readers, let them remember that even a highly paid writer and lecturer in his day could not hope to get money as fast or as surely as a lawyer, or a physician, not to speak of the plutocrats he hated but may also have envied. He did it by driving himself to hard work, and a man who has to drive himself to get money after middle age may resent the fact, without being able to stop.

Writing about the teaching profession, Leacock deplored the poor wages that it brought in his time, and said that a teacher ought to be able to enjoy some of the sweets of life and to feel "as good as anybody else." The phrase makes us pause. Did Leacock, with his very large public and his substantial income, ever feel "as good as anybody else" in his own estimation? He represents professors, in his writings, as amiable, unworldly men, devoted to learning and firm in their scholarly integrity, but as men laughed at by the world at large for earnings that hardly rose above those of the clergy. I do not suggest that Leacock's measure of success was money: I do suggest that somewhere deep inside him lurked a dissatisfaction with himself that sought a justification, and that want of money served him as a partial, never wholly satisfactory, justification. Read his work carefully and with attention to the chronology of its appearance, and see if there does not arise from the pages the image of a man who was, in part, angry, desirous of rewards that life did not provide, and too often contemptuous toward his readers. Every humorist becomes aware that many of his readers are stupid people; it is the fate of those who minister to the Belly and the Members.

In part – the qualification is important. Another element in his character was a quality of boisterous high spirits, of the clubman, the fisherman, and the genial host. But these things were balanced by depressed moods in which he could be disagreeable and – I quote a man who knew him – "often damned rude." He knew many people but gave his friendship sparingly, and when he did so it was with a demand for loyalty and submission that – again I depend on evidence of men who knew him – was hard on the friend. And his hospitality could be marred by outbursts of temper about bad service, followed by a wholesale discharging of the servants – who were hired back next morning at increased wages.

A man whose flash-point was as low as Leacock's might be dismissed as irascible if he were not also a wit of great reputation. A humorist is a humorist for the same reason that a poet is a poet; he has a disposition of mind, a bias of sensibility, that makes him so, and when Leacock set to work to explain to the readers of *How To Write* a method of writing humour, he must have known how hopeless the task was, for he was trying to tell them how to be like himself. His own best advice about writing was contained in a single sentence: "Writing is simply jotting down the things that occur to you; the jotting presents no problem, but the occurring is a different matter." The occurring, if the writer aspires to be a humorist, seems to be a matter of a tension in the mind that calls for discharge, and if we are to believe Sigmund Freud's theory, set forth in *Wit and Its Relation to The Unconscious*, this tension had its origin in a sense of the intolerability of things as they appear and a desire to present them in another light. The light the humorist seeks to shed is nothing less than the light of truth.

Freud also suggests that the humorist seeks to take us back momentarily to the intellectual freedom of childhood, when everything was fresh to us, and freshly apprehended; if something seemed stupid or unimportant to us, we said so without regard for what the adult world thought; so also, if something seemed delightful we dwelt upon it, even if adults thought it trivial or inopportune or possibly disgusting. The humorist does this, and part of the price he pays for his gift is that he is thought childish, or a trifler, when we have been snatched back into the solemnity of the adult world. People of conventional and immobile intellect are apt to think tragedy more important than it is, and comedy less important than it is, because this accords with what they consider an adult view of life. People of greater intellectual capacity, of broader emotional scope, value tragedy and comedy alike because they extend the range of feeling and understanding instead of conforming to some already established canon of value. Leacock at his best is a great humorist because he speaks the truth and extends our vision.

An aspect of his work in which he shows particular individuality is his use of language. At his best he writes with a deceptive simplicity because he writes in the rhythm of his own speech as he used it on the lecture platform. He did not always speak simply; his university lectures were delivered in the language suited to the complexity of his subject, and when he made a political speech, he expected his hearers to understand the appropriate terms. But when he lectured as a humorist he spoke with a simplicity that went beyond that of Mark Twain, who had a tradition of Southern eloquence behind him, even though he scorned its baroque excesses. Leacock spoke like a Canadian – simply, in sentences usually brief, avoiding slang but by no means unconscious of the flavour and impact of simple words used in unfamiliar contexts. When we read his best work, we hear the same rhythms; he even writes down the interrogative "eh?" which is characteristic of so much Canadian vernacular. This is why such a piece as "My Financial Career" is so much funnier read aloud than read with the eye alone. As it approaches its climax it brings a laugh at the end of every sentence. Such speaker's prose is not his alone, but as he used it in his best work it is inimitable. It depends on a skill in choice of words, and a concealed elegance in placing them, which produces effects far beyond the common speech it so brilliantly suggests.

It looks easy and foolish people thought it easy. An English reviewer once wrote of him: "What is there, after all, in Professor Leacock's humour but a rather ingenious mixture of hyperbole and myosis?" His comment is a criticism of the critic:

> The man was right. How he stumbled upon this trade secret, I do not know. But I am willing to admit, since the truth is out, that it has been my custom in preparing an article of a humorous nature, to go down to the cellar and mix up half a gallon of myosis with a pint of hyperbole. If I want to give the article a decidedly literary flavour, I find it well to put in about half a pint of paresis. The whole thing is amazingly simple.

This is the real Leacock. When he wrote of Dickens, "You encourage a comic man too much and he gets silly," he had not yet written *How To Write*, and we may think it a pity he did not remember this true and pungent comment. So too, when he wrote, "Praise and appreciation, the very soil in which art best flourishes, may prompt too rank a growth," he might have been offering a criticism of his own voluminous, uninspired production.

Praise and appreciation were certainly lavished on him in generous measure, though not so freely in Canada as in England and the United States. The late Dr. Lorne Pierce, writing about Literature in the *Encyclopaedia of Canada* could say: "He is a kindly critic of the foibles and absurdities of humanity. He has created no outstanding character, being content to show up, with his ridiculous verbiage and boisterous fooling, the nonsense of the common people about him." Dr. Pierce missed the creation of one extraordinary character, which was the public mask of Stephen Leacock himself, one of the great geniuses of the lecture platform. We may find his use of language ridiculous in some of his poorer work; it is true that he seemed to think that an interjection like "ha ha!" was funnier if spelled "Har har!", and that a mere fellow became a darling of Comic Spirit if he were called a "feller," but his best work has a prose magic, rooted in speech, that Dr. Pierce has missed. A truer judgement was that offered by Peter McArthur in his volume on Leacock in the "Makers of Canadian Literature" series, in 1923: "As matters stand he is one of the truest interpreters of American and

Canadian life we have had." This was succeeded by a prophecy that was fulfilled in *The Boy I Left Behind Me*: "by giving free play to all his powers he may finally win recognition as a broad and sympathetic interpreter of life as a whole." Canada was not a kindly soil for a writer in Leacock's day; the watchers and the holy ones who were on the lookout for the Great Canadian Novel were patronizing toward ridiculous verbiage and boisterous fooling, but there were a few who kept an eye on what was really happening. McArthur was one of them, as was also Pelham Edgar, a judicious critic who could see what Leacock was, as well as what he failed to be. Perhaps it is unfair to expect a country, very new to literature and conscious of the high achievements of the mother country and of its great neighbour, to value fully so original a man of letters as was Leacock. He was admired, but it is doubtful if his stature was recognized.

In his perfunctory little book about Canadian literature, *O Canada*, the American critic Edmund Wilson describes Leacock's writings as "slapdash buffooneries," but says that they display "a Canadian violence"; he has missed the humour, for he has never written perceptively about humour and seems to have none of his own, but his comment on the violence is important. Leacock is violent, however much he may write in his off hours about "the kindly contemplation of the incongruities of life." His violence springs from a tension in the mind that characterizes many Canadians, and which they control with obvious effort. Leacock had more of it than most of us, and he found a way of giving it vent that was acceptable, and that could even be dismissed by the unwitting as "boisterous fooling," or "slapdash buffoonery." Leacock is violent as Charlie Chaplin is violent; under the clowning works a vigorous, turbulent spirit, whose mellowest productions leave always on the palate a hint of the basic brimstone.

His place in the literature of Canada must seem ambiguous to readers who do not study his work with care. He wrote most of his magazine pieces for publication abroad, and it is not surprising that he did not attach them unmistakably to Canadian settings; what is surprising is how often we, as readers, are able to do so. *Sunshine Sketches* is as Canadian as any book that was ever written, and it has been understood and cherished in every country where English is read. As Owen Seaman so truly said when Leacock lectured in London, his humour was British by birth and American by adoption; quite often, also, people remembered that he was a professor in a Canadian university. But as we read the books published during the First World War and the articles he published during the war of 1939-45, we are aware of a quality which is neither English nor American; some of it is bad Leacock, but the quality of concern is strongly Canadian. All his life Leacock was an eloquent and devoted apologist for the British Empire and its successor, the British Commonwealth, and he always wrote and spoke not as an Englishman, but as a Canadian. There was no doubt in his mind as to the country of his allegiance, which he thought of as part of a great family of nations. It would be unjust to say that he was ahead of his time in his sense of Canada's national entity; we may say with conviction, however, that his expression of what he felt on the lecture platform and in his writing was cast in a mode that was still unfamiliar in Canada and today, when patriotism is out of fashion, is no nearer comprehension.

Patriotism was part of the large simplicity of his mind. He was a man of strongly masculine cast of intellect and feeling, and strength, generosity, and fidelity were native to him. This great area of force was compensated for by a weakness of sympathy with everything that might be called feminine in art or life, and by a lack of sensibility in his relationships with other people. But he was a man to whom less vigorous personalities were attracted, and from whom they drew sustenance; if some of them were occasionally wounded by the giant to whom they had attached themselves, not all the blame must rest on him; it is not fair to expect a giant to be a model of compassion. Leacock possessed qualities that would have made him a leader in several walks of life other than that which he chose, or toward which circumstances inclined him. As a leader, it was not in him to doubt his convictions, or to be tender toward excessive scruple in others. As a Tory Imperialist he made a long pilgrimage in the realm of political opinion from the days of his youth to his old age, but he did not become a different man. In judging his work we must bear in mind that the Canada he saw and of which he wrote was not the Canada of today, and that it is the passing of time, rather than any falsity in his mind, that makes some of his opinions strange.

There is much still to be discovered about his life, but we need expect no more substantial discoveries about his work from letters or occasional pieces. The volumes we have show him as a man of intellectually conservative opinions, preserved in the face of doubts that contradicted them – a

Feast of Stephen

conflict between mind and emotion not uncommon among writers. They show a sardonic apprehension of experience that goes far beyond the cat-scratching of cynicism, and which was under the fitful control of a strong native kindliness, supported in its turn by a sense of justice which was allied to his academic preoccupation. They show a classical training at odds with a romantic tendency to accept personal judgement as of final validity. And they show a man who, despite much worldly success, never was able to rid his heart of the ache of early wounds.

Yet, when this has been said, the most important quality remains. Leacock was a genius in that he possessed the power to do in an inimitably personal way what very few people can do at all. He was a man set apart, who lived, worked and felt on an ampler scale than those who lacked his gift. What has been said here, though it has sometimes dwelt on what was negative or less than admirable in his life and work, has at all times been meant as a grateful celebration of that gift, which enriched his country and all who are concerned with literature in the land he claimed as his own.

ROBERTSON DAVIES.

Selected bibliography

Adventures of the Far North, A Chronicle of the Frozen Seas (Toronto, Glasgow: Brook & Company, 1914). Chronicles of Canada series, v.20.

Afternoons in Utopia; Tales of the New Time (Toronto: The Macmillan Company of Canada, Ltd., 1932).

Arcadian Adventures with the Idle Rich (London: John Lane, 1914).*

Baldwin, Lafontaine, Hincks; Responsible Government (Toronto: Morang & Company, Ltd., 1907).

Behind the Beyond and Other Contributions to Human Knowledge (London: John Lane, 1913).* Illustrated by A. H. Fish.

The Best of Leacock (Toronto: McClelland and Stewart, 1958). Edited and introduced by J. B. Priestley.

The Boy I Left Behind Me (Garden City, New York; Doubleday & Company, Inc., 1946).

Charles Dickens, His Life and Work (London: P. Davies, 1933).

College Days (New York: Dodd, Mead & Company, 1923).

The Dry Pickwick and Other Incongruities (London: John Lane, The Bodley Head, 1932).

Economic Prosperity in the British Empire (Toronto: The Macmillan Company of Canada, Ltd., 1930).

Elements of Political Science (Boston and New York: Houghton, Mifflin and Company, 1906).

Essays and Literary Studies (New York, John Lane Company; London, John Lane, The Bodley Head; Toronto, S. B. Gundy, 1916).

Frenzied Fiction (London, John Lane, The Bodley Head; New York, John Lane Company, 1918).*

Funny Pieces; A Book of Random Sketches (New York: Dodd, Mead & Company, 1936).

Further Foolishness; Sketches and Satires on the Follies of the Day (New York, John Lane Company; London, John Lane, The Bodley Head; Toronto, S. B. Gundy, 1916).*

The Garden of Folly (Toronto: S. B. Gundy, 1924).

Happy Stories, Just to Laugh At (New York: Dodd, Mead & Company, 1943).

Hellements of Hickonomics in Hiccoughs of Verse Done in Our Social Planning Mill (New York: Dodd, Mead & Company, 1936).

Here Are My Lectures and Stories (New York: Dodd, Mead & Company, 1937).

The Hohenzollerns in America; with The Bolsheviks in Berlin and Other Impossibilities (London, John Lane, The Bodley Head; New York, John Lane Company, 1919).

How to Write (New York: Dodd, Mead & Company, 1943).

Humour and Humanity; An Introduction to the Study of Humour (London: Thornton Butterworth, Ltd., 1937).

Humor: Its Theory and Technique, with Examples and Samples; A Book of Discovery (Toronto; Dodd, Mead & Company, [c1935)].

The Iron Man & the Tin Woman, with Other Such Futurities; A Book of Little Sketches of To-day and To-morrow (New York: Dodd, Mead & Company, 1929).

Last Leaves (Toronto: McClelland & Stewart, [c1945]).

Laugh Parade; A New Collection of the Wit and Humor of Stephen Leacock (New York: Dodd, Mead & Company, 1940).

Laugh with Leacock; an Anthology of the best works of Stephen Leacock. (New York: Dodd Mead & Company, 1930).

Lincoln Frees the Slaves (New York: G. P. Putnam's Sons, 1934).

Literary Lapses; A Book of Sketches (Montreal: Gazette Printing Company, Ltd., 1910).*

Mark Twain ([London]: Peter Davies, Ltd., 1932).

Model Memoirs and Other Sketches from Simple to Serious (New York: Dodd, Mead & Company, 1938).

Moonbeams from the Larger Lunacy (New York: John Lane Company, 1915).*

My Discovery of England (London: John Lane, 1922).*

My Discovery of the West; A Discussion of East and West in Canada (Toronto: Thomas Allen, 1937).

My Remarkable Uncle and Other Sketches (New York: Dodd, Mead & Company, 1942).*

Nonsense Novels (London, John Lane; New York, John Lane Company, 1911).*

Over the Footlights (Toronto: S. B. Gundy, 1923).

The Perfect Salesman (New York: Robert M. McBride & Company, [1934]). Edited by E. V. Knox.

"Q"; A Farce in One Act (New York: S. French, c1915). By Stephen Leacock and Basil Macdonald Hastings.

Short Circuits (Toronto: The Macmillan Company of Canada, Ltd., [1928]).*

Sunshine Sketches of a Little Town (London, John Lane, The Bodley Head; New York, John Lane Company; Toronto, Bell & Cockburn, 1912).*

Too Much College; or, Education Eating Up Life, with

Kindred Essays in Education and Humour (New York: Dodd, Mead & Company, 1939).

The Unsolved Riddle of Social Justice (New York, John Lane Company; London, John Lane, The Bodley Head; Toronto, S. B. Gundy, 1920).

Wet Wit and Dry Humour, Distilled from the Pages of Stephen Leacock (New York: Dodd, Mead & Company, 1931).

Winnowed Wisdom; A New Book of Humour (New York: Dodd, Mead & Company, 1926).

Winsome Winnie, and Other New Nonsense Novels (Toronto, S. B. Gundy; London, John Lane, The Bodley Head; New York, John Lane Company, 1920).

ARTICLES AND BOOKS ABOUT STEPHEN LEACOCK

CAMERON, D. A. "The Enchanted Houses: Leacock's Irony," *Canadian Literature* 23 (Winter, 1965), pp. 31-44.
Faces of Leacock: An Appreciation (Toronto: Ryerson, 1967).

CLEMENTS, C. "An Evening with Stephen Leacock," *Catholic World* 159 (June, 1944), pp. 236-241.

COLLINS, J. P. "Professor Leacock, Ph.D.; Savant and Humorist," *BKMN* (London) 51 (Nov., 1916), pp. 39-44. Also in *Living Age* 291 (Dec. 30, 1916), pp. 800 ff.

CURRY, RALPH L. "Stephen Butler Leacock, A Check-List," *Bulletin of Bibliography* 22 (January-April, 1958), pp. 106-109. Supplements Lomer's *Check List.*
"Stephen Leacock: Humorist and Humanist" (Garden City: Doubleday, 1959).
Introduction to *Arcadian Adventures with the Idle Rich* (Toronto: McClelland and Stewart, 1959), pp. vii-xi.

DAVIES, ROBERTSON Introduction to *Literary Lapses* (Toronto: McClelland and Stewart, 1957), pp. vii-ix.
"Stephen Leacock," *Our Living Tradition,* First Series, ed. Claude T. Bissell (Toronto: University of Toronto Press, 1957), pp. 128-149.
"On Stephen Leacock," *Masks of Fiction,* ed. A. J. M. Smith (Toronto: McClelland & Stewart, 1961), pp. 93-114.
Introduction to *Moonbeams from the Larger Lunacy* (Toronto: McClelland and Stewart, 1964), pp. vii-x.

DAY, J. P. "Professor Leacock at McGill," *Canadian Journal of Economics* 10 (May, 1944), pp. 226-228.

EDGAR, PELHAM "Stephen Leacock," *Queen's Quarterly* 53 (Summer, 1946), pp. 173-184. Reprinted in his *Across My Path,* ed. Northrop Frye (Toronto: Ryerson, 1952), pp. 90-98. Also in *Our Sense of Identity* ed. Malcolm Ross (Toronto: Ryerson, 1954), pp. 136-146.

GILLISS, K. E. "Stephen Leacock as a Satirist" (Thesis, University of New Brunswick, 1957).

INNIS, HAROLD "Stephen Butler Leacock (1869-1944)," *Canadian Journal of Economics* 10 (May, 1944), pp. 216-226.

LOMER, GERHARD R. *Stephen Leacock: A Check-List and Index of His Writings* (Ottawa: National Library, 1954).

LOWER, ARTHUR "The Mariposa Belle," *Queen's Quarterly* 58 (Summer, 1951), pp. 220-226.

MCARTHUR, PETER *Stephen Leacock* (Toronto: Ryerson, 1923).

MASSON, T. L. "Stephen Leacock," in his *Our American Humorists* (New York: Dodd Mead, 1931), pp. 209-229.

MIKES, GEORGE "Stephen Leacock," in his *Eight Humorists* (London: Wingate, 1954), pp. 41-65.

NIMMO, BARBARA Preface to *Last Leaves* (New York: Dodd Mead, 1945), pp. vii-xx.

PACEY, DESMOND "Leacock as a Satirist," *Queen's Quarterly* 58 (Summer, 1951), pp. 208-219.

PHELPS, ARTHUR L. "Stephen Leacock," in his *Canadian Writers* (Toronto: McClelland & Stewart, 1951), pp. 70-76.

ROSS, DAVID W. "Stephen Leacock, Scholar and Humorist" (Thesis, Columbia University, 1947).

ROSS, MALCOLM Introduction to *Sunshine Sketches of a Little Town* (Toronto: McClelland and Stewart, 1960), pp. ix-xvi.

SANDWELL, B. K. "He Made Humour Almost Respectable," *Canadian Author and Bookman* 23 (Fall, 1947), pp. 13-16.

"Here Stephen Leacock Lives and Writes," *Saturday Night* 58 (October 10, 1942), p. 4.

"Leacock Recalled: How the 'Sketches' Started," *Saturday Night* 67 (August 23, 1952), p. 7.

"Leacock for Canadians," *Saturday Night* 64 (February 1, 1949), pp. 1-2.

"Stephen Butler Leacock, 1869-1944," Royal Society of Canada *Proceedings and Transactions* (Third Series) 38 (1944), pp. 105-106.

SEDGWICK, G. G. "Stephen Leacock as a Man of Letters," *University of Toronto Quarterly* 15 (October, 1945), pp. 17-26.

WATT, F. W. "Critic or Entertainer?" *Canadian Literature* 5 (Summer, 1960), pp. 33-42.

WATTERS, R. E. "A Special Tang: Stephen Leacock's Canadian Humour," *Canadian Literature* 5 (Summer, 1960), pp. 21-32. Also in the revised edition of *Canadian Anthology* eds. Klinck and Watters (Toronto: Gage, 1966), pp. 540-547.

Starred titles available in New Canadian Library series.

Feast
of
Stephen

Selections
from
Stephen Leacock

Life on the Old Farm

I enjoy the distinction, until very recently a sort of recognized title of nobility in Canada and the United States, of having been "raised on the old farm." Till recently, I say, this was the acknowledged path towards future greatness, the only way to begin. The biographies of virtually all our great men for three or four generations show them as coming from the farm. The location of the "old home farm" was anywhere from Nova Scotia to out beyond Iowa, but in its essence and idea it was always the same place. I once described it in a book of verse which I wrote as a farewell to economics, which was so clever that no one could read it and which I may therefore quote with novelty now.

> The Homestead Farm, way back upon the Wabash,
>   Or on the Yockikenny,
>   Or somewhere up near Albany – the Charm
>   Was not confined to one, for there were many.
> There when the earliest Streak of Sunrise ran,
> The Farmer dragged the Horses from their Dream
> With "Get up, Daisy" and "Gol darn yer, Fan,"
> Had scarcely snapped the Tugs and Britching than
> The furious Hayrack roared behind the team.
>   All day the Hay
>   Was drawn that way
>   Hurled in the Mow
>   Up high – and how!
> Till when the ending Twilight came, the loaded Wain
> With its last, greatest Load turned Home again.
>   The Picture of it rises to his Eye
>   Sitting beside his Father, near the Sky.

I admit that within the last generation or so, in softer times of multiplying luxury, men of eminence have been raised in a sickly sort of way in the cities themselves, have got their strength from high-school athletics, instead of at the woodpile and behind the harrows, and their mental culture by reading a hundred books once instead of one book a hundred times. But I am talking of an earlier day.

It was a condition, of course, that one must be raised on the old farm and then succeed in getting off it. Those who stayed on it turned into rustics, into "hicks" and "rubes," into those upstate characters which are the delight of the comic stage. You had your choice! Stay there and turn into a hick; get out and be a great man. But the strange thing is that they all come back. They leave the old farm as boys so gladly, so happy to get away from its dull routine, its meaningless sunrise and sunset, its empty fresh winds over its fields, the silence of the bush – to get away into the clatter and effort of life, into the crowd. Then, as the years go by, they come to realize that at a city desk and in a city apartment they never see the sunrise and the sunset, have forgotten what the sky looks like at night and where the Great Dipper is, and find nothing in the angry gusts of wind or the stifling heat of the city streets that corresponds to the wind over the empty fields . . . so they go back, or they think they do, back to the old farm. Only they rebuild it, but not with an ax but with an architect. They make it a great country mansion with flagstoned piazzas and festooned pergolas – and it isn't the old farm any more. You can't have it both ways.

But as I say, I had my qualifying share, six years of the old farm – after I came out as a child of six from England – in an isolation which in these days of radio and transport is unknown upon the globe.

As explained in the first chapter, I was brought out by my mother from England to Canada as the third of her six children in 1876 on the steamship *Sarmatian,* Liverpool to Montreal, to join my father who had gone ahead and taken up a farm. The *Sarmatian* was one, was practically the last one, of those grand old vessels of the Allan Line which combined steam with the towering masts, the cloud of canvas, the maze of ropes and rigging of a full-rigged three-masted ship. She was in her day a queen of the ocean, that last word which always runs on to another sentence. She had been built in 1871, had had the honour of serving the queen as a troopship for the Ashanti war and the further honour of carrying the queen's daughter to Canada as the wife of the Marquis of Lorne, the governor general. No wonder that in my recollection of her the *Sarmatian* seemed grand beyond belief and carried a wealth of memories of the voyage of which I have already spoken. For years I used to feel as if I would "give anything" to see the *Sarmatian* again. "Give anything" at that stage of my finance meant, say, anything up to five dollars – anyway, a whole lot. And then it happened years and years after, when I had gone to Montreal to teach at McGill (it was in 1902), that I saw in the papers that the *Sarmatian* was in port; in fact I found that she still came in regularly all season and would be back again before navigation closed. So I never saw her. I meant to but I never did. When I read a little later that the old ship had been broken up I felt that I would have "given anything" (ten dollars then) to have seen her.

In those days most people still came up, as we did in 1876, by river steamer from Montreal to Toronto. At Kingston we saw the place all decked with flags and were told that it was the "Twenty-fourth of May." We asked what that meant, because in those days they didn't keep "Queen's Birthday" as a holiday in England. They kept Coronation Day with a great ringing of bells, but whether there was any more holiday to it than bell ringing I don't remember. But, as we were presently to learn, the "Twenty-fourth" was at that time the great Upper Canada summer holiday of the year; Dominion Day was still too new to have got set. There wasn't any Labour Day or any Civic Holiday.

From Toronto we took a train north to Newmarket; a funny train, it seemed to us, all open and quite unlike the little English carriages, cut into compartments that set the fields spinning round when you looked out of the window. Newmarket in 1876 was a well-established country town, in fact, as they said, "quite a place." It still is. It was at that time the place from which people went by the country roads to the south side of Lake Simcoe, the township of Georgina, to which at that time there was no railway connection. From Newmarket my father and his hired man were to drive us the remaining thirty miles to reach the old farm. They had for it two wagons, a lumber wagon and a "light" wagon. A light wagon was lighter than a lumber wagon, but that's all you could say about it – it is like those histories which professors call "short" histories. They might have been longer. So away we went along the zigzag roads, sometimes along a good stretch that would allow the horses to break into a heavy attempt at a trot, at other times ploughing through sand, tugging uphill, or hauling over corduroy roads of logs through thick swamps where the willow and alder bushes

almost met overhead and where there was "no room to pass."
On the lift of the hills we could see about us a fine rolling
country, all woods, broken with farms, and here and there
in the distance on the north horizon great flecks of water that
were Lake Simcoe. And so on, at a pace of four or five miles
an hour, till as the day closed in we went over a tumbled
bridge with a roaring milldam and beyond it a village, the
village of Sutton – two mills, two churches, and quite a main
street, with three taverns. My father told us that this was our
own village, a gift very lightly received by us children after
memories of Porchester and Liverpool and the *Sarmatian*.
My mother told me years afterwards that to her it was a
heartbreak. Beyond the village, my father told us, we were
on our home road – another dubious gift, for it was as heavy
as ever, with a great cedar swamp a mile through in the
centre, all corduroy and willows and marsh and water; beyond that up a great hill with more farmhouses, and so
across some fields, to a wind-swept hill space with a jumble
of frame buildings and log barns and outhouses, and there
we were at the old farm, on a six-year unbroken sentence.

The country round our farm was new in the sense that
forty years before it was unbroken wilderness and old in the
sense that farm settlers, when they began to come, had come
in quickly. Surveyors had marked out roads. The part of the
bush that was easy to clear was cleared off in one generation,
log houses built, and one or two frame ones, so that in the
sense the country in its outline was just as it is now: only at
that time it was more bush than farms, now more farms than
the shrunken remnant of bush. And of course in 1876 a lot
of old primeval trees, towering hemlocks and birch, were still
standing. The last of the great bush fires that burned them
out was in the summer when we came, the bush all burning,
the big trees falling in masses of spark and flame, the sky all
bright, and the people gathered from all around to beat out
the shower of sparks that fell in the stubble fields . . .

This country around Lake Simcoe (we were four miles to
the south of it and out of the sight of it), beautiful and
fertile as it is, had never been settled in the old colonial days.
The French set up missions there among the Hurons (northwest of the lake), but they were wiped out in the great
Iroquois massacre of 1649 in the martyrdom of the Fathers
Lalemant and Brébeuf. The tourist of today sees from his
flying car the road signs of "Martyr's Shrine" intermingled
with the "Hot Dogs" and "Joe's Garage." After the massacre

the French never came back. The Iroquois danger kept the country empty, as it did all western Ontario. Nor did the United Empire Loyalists come here. They settled along the St. Lawrence and the Bay of Quinte and Niagara and Lake Erie, but the Lake Simcoe country remained till that century closed as empty as it is beautiful.

Settlement came after the "Great War" ended with Waterloo and world peace, and a flock of British emigrants went out to the newer countries. Among them were many disbanded soldiers and sailors and officers with generous grants of land. These were what were called in England "good" people, meaning people of the "better" class but not good enough to stay home, which takes money. With them came adherents and servants and immigrants at large, but all good people in the decent sense of the word, as were all the people round our old farm no matter how poor they were. The entry of these people to the Lake Simcoe country was made possible by Governor Simcoe's opening of Yonge Street, north from Toronto to the Holland River. It was at first just a horse track through the bush, presently a rough roadway connecting Toronto (York) with the Holland River, and then, by cutting the corner of Lake Simcoe with the Georgian Bay and thus westward to the Upper Lakes, a line of communication safe from American invasion. It was part of Governor Simcoe's preoccupation over the defense of Upper Canada, which bore such good fruit in its unforeseen results of new settlement.

So the settlers, once over the waters of Lake Simcoe, found their way along its shore, picked out the likely places, the fine high ground, the points overlooking the lake. Here within a generation arose comfortable lake-shore homes, built by people with a certain amount of money, aided by people with no money but glad to work for wages for a time, till they could do better. From the first the settlement was cast in an aristocratic mould such as had been Governor Simcoe's dream for all his infant colony. Simcoe was long since gone by this time. He left Canada in 1796 and died in England in 1806. But the mark that he set on Upper Canada wore faint only with time and is not yet obliterated. Simcoe planned a constitution and a colony to be an "image and transcript" of England itself. An established church and an aristocracy must be the basis of it. To Simcoe a democrat was a dangerous Jacobin and a dissenter a snivelling hypocrite. He despised people who would sit down to eat with their own servants, as even "good" people began to do in

Upper Canada; "Fellows of one table," he called them, and he wanted nothing to do with them in his government. Others shared his views, and hence that queer touch of make-believe, or real aristocracy, that was then characteristic of Simcoe's York (Toronto) and that helped to foster the Canadian rebellion of 1837.

So after the first "aristocracy" houses were built on the lake shore of Georgina Township settlers began to move up to the higher ground behind it, better land and cheaper. For the lake, for being on the water, most of them cared nothing. They wanted to get away from it. The lake shore was cold. It is strange to think that now you can buy all of that farm-land you want at about thirty or forty dollars an acre, but an acre down at the lake shore is worth, say, a couple of thousand, and you can't get it anyway.

Our own farm with its buildings was, I will say, the damnedest place I ever saw. The site was all right, for the slow slope of the hillside west and south gave a view over miles of country and a view of the sunset only appreciated when lost. But the house! Someone had built a cedar log house and then covered it round with clapboard, and then someone else had added three rooms stuck along the front with more clapboard, effectually keeping all the sunlight out. Even towards the sunset there were no windows, only the half glass top of a side door. A cookhouse and a woodshed were stuck on behind. Across a grass yard were the stable, cedar logs plastered up, and the barns, cedar logs loose and open, and a cart shed and a henhouse, and pigsties and all that goes with a farm. To me as a child the farm part seemed just one big stink. It does still: the phew! of the stable – not so bad as the rest; the unspeakable cowshed, sunk in the dark below a barn, beyond all question of light or ventilation, like a mediæval oubliette; the henhouse, never cleaned and looking like a guano-deposit island off the coast of Chile, in which the hens lived if they could and froze dead if they couldn't; the pigsties, on the simple Upper Canada fashion of a log pen and a shelter behind, about three feet high. Guano had nothing on them.

We presently completed our farmhouse to match the growing family by adding a new section on the far side of it, built of frame lumber only, with lath and plaster and no logs, thin as cardboard and cold as a refrigerator. Everything froze when the thermometer did. We took for granted that the water would freeze in the pitchers every night and the windowpanes cover up with frost, not that the old farm was not heated. It had had originally a big stone fireplace in the original log house, but as with all the fireplaces built of stone out of the fields without firebrick, as the mortar began to dry out the fireplace would set the house on fire. That meant getting up on the roof (it wasn't far) with buckets of water and putting it out. My father and the hired man got so tired putting out the house on fire that we stopped using the fireplace and had only stoves, box stoves that burned hemlock, red hot in ten minutes with the dampers open. You could be as warm as you liked, according to distance, but the place was never the same two hours running. There were, I think, nine stoves in all; cutting wood was endless. I quote again from my forgotten book.

> Winter stopped not the Work; it never could.
> Behold the Furious Farmer splitting Wood.
> The groaning Hemlock creaks at every Blow
> "Hit her again, Dad, she's just got to go."
> > And up he picks
> > The Hemlock sticks
> > Out of the snow.

For light we had three or four coal-oil lamps, but being just from England, where they were unknown, we were afraid of them. We used candles made on the farm from tallow poured into a mould, guttering damn things, to be snuffed all the time and apt to droop over in the middle. It is hardly credible to me now, but I know it is a fact that when my brother and I sat round a table doing our lessons or drawing and painting pictures, all the light we had was one tallow candle in the middle of the table. It should have ruined our eyesight, but it didn't. I don't think any of us under fifty wore spectacles; just as the ill-cooked food of the farm, the heavy doughy bread, the awful pork and pickles should have ruined our digestions but couldn't. Boys on the farm who go after the cattle at six in the morning are in the class of the iron dogs beside a city step.

My father's farm – one hundred acres, the standard pattern – was based on what is called mixed farming – that is, wheat and other grains, hay, pasture, cattle, a few sheep and pigs and hens, roots for winter, garden for summer and wood to cut in the bush. The only thing to sell was wheat, the false hope of the Ontario farmer of the seventies, always lower in the yield than what one calculated (if you calculated low it went lower) and always (except once in a happy year) lower than what it had to be to make it pay. The other odd grains we had to sell brought nothing much, nor the cattle, poor lean things of the prebreeding days that survived their awful cowshed. My father knew nothing about farming, and the hired man, "Old Tommy," a Yorkshireman who had tried a bush farm of his own and failed, still less. My father alternated furious industry with idleness and drinking, and in spite of my mother having a small income of her own from England, the farm drifted onto the rocks and the family into debt. Presently there was a mortgage, the interest on which being like a chain around my father's neck, and later on mine. Indeed, these years of the late 1870s were the hard times of Ontario farming, with mortages falling due like snowflakes.

Farming in Ontario, in any case, was then and still is an alternating series of mortgages and prosperity following on like the waves of the sea. Anyone of my experience could drive you through the present farm country and show you (except that it would bore you to sleep) the mark of the successive waves like geological strata. Here on our right is the remains of what was the original log house of a settler: you can tell it from the remains of a barn, because if you look close you can see that it had a top story, or part of one, like the loft where Abraham Lincoln slept. You will see, too, a section of its outline that was once a window. Elsewhere, perhaps on the same farm, but still standing, is an old frame house that was built by mortgaging the log house. This one may perhaps be boarded up and out of use because it was discarded when wheat went to two dollars and fifty cents a bushel in the Crimean War and the farmer, suddenly enriched, was able to add another mortgage and built a brick house – those real brick houses that give the motorist the impression that all farmers are rich. So they were – during the Crimean War. Later on, and reflecting the boom years of the closing nineties and the opening century, are the tall hip-roofed barns with stone and cement basements below for cattle and silos at the side, which give the impression that all farmers are scientists – only they aren't; it's just more mortgages.

Such has been the background of Ontario farming for one hundred years.

Our routine on the farm, as children, was to stay on it. We were too little to wander, and even the nearest neighbours were half a mile away. So we went nowhere except now and then, as a treat, into Sutton village, and on Sunday

Feast of Stephen

to the church on the lake shore. Practically, except for school, we stayed at home all the time – years and years.

There was, a mile away, a school (School Section No. 3, Township of Georgina) of the familiar type of the "little red schoolhouse" that has helped to make America. It was a plain frame building, decently lighted, with a yard and a pump and a woodpile, in fact all the accessories that went with the academic life of School Section No. 3. The boys and girls who went there were the children of decent people (there were no others in the township), poor, but not exactly aware of it. In summer the boys went barefoot. We didn't – a question of caste and thistles. You have to begin it at three years old to get the feel for it.

There were two teachers, a man teacher and a lady teacher, and it was all plain and decent and respectable, and the education first class, away ahead of the dame-school stuff in England. All of the education was right to the point – reading, spelling, writing, arithmetic, geography – with no fancy, silly subjects such as disfigure our present education even at its beginning and run riot in the college at the top. Things about the school that were unsanitary were things then so customary that even we children from England found nothing wrong. We spit on our slates to clean them with the side of our hand. We all drank out of the same tin mug in the schoolyard. The boys and girls were together in classes, never outside.

The only weak spot in the system of the little red schoolhouse was that the teachers were not permanent, not men engaged in teaching making it their lifework, like the Scottish "dominie" who set his mark upon Scotland. You can never have a proper system of national education without teachers who make teaching their lifework, take a pride in it as a chosen profession, and are so circumstanced as to be as good as anybody – I mean as anything around. In the lack of this lies the great fault in our Canadian secondary education, all the way up to college.

So it was with the country schools of 1876. The teachers were young men who came and went, themselves engaged in the long stern struggle of putting themselves through college, for which their teaching was only a stepping-stone. An arduous struggle it was. A schoolteacher (they were practically all men; the girl teachers were just appendages to the picture) got a salary of three hundred dollars to four hundred dollars a year. Call it four hundred dollars. During his ten months a year of teaching he paid ten dollars a month for his board and washing. I don't suppose that his clothes cost him more than fifty dollars a year, and all his other extras of every kind certainly not more than another fifty. For in those days, after necessaries were paid for, there was nothing to spend money on. The teacher never drank. Not that he didn't want to, but every drink cost money, five cents, and he hadn't got it. If a teacher did begin to drink and did start to loaf around the taverns, it undermined the sternness of his life's purpose as a slow leak undermines a dam. It became easier to drink than to save money; he felt rich instead of poor, and presently, as the years went by, he drank himself out of this purpose altogether, quit schoolteaching, went north – to the lumber shanties or worked in a sawmill – living life downhill, marked out still, by the wreck of his education, as a man who had once been a teacher and still quoted poetry when he was tight.

But most, practically all, stuck right at it, saving, say, two hundred dollars a year towards college. And this is what college cost, college being the University of Toronto. The fees were forty dollars a year (say sixty dollars in medicine), and board and lodging in the mean drab houses of the side streets where the poorer students lived cost three dollars a week, and washing, I think, twenty-five cents a week. They washed anything then for five cents, even a full-dress shirt, and anyway the student hadn't got a full-dress shirt. College books in those days cost about ten dollars a year. There were no college activities that cost money, nothing to join that wanted five dollars for joining it, no cafeterias to spend money in, since a student ate three times a day at his boardinghouse and that was the end of it. There was no money to be spent on college girls, because at that time there were no college girls to spend money on. Homer says that the beauty of Helen of Troy launched a thousand ships (meaning made that much trouble). The attraction of the college girl was to launch about a thousand dollars – added to college expenses.

But all that was far, far away in 1876, and a student's college budget for the eight months of the session, including his clothes and his travel expenses and such extras as even the humblest and sternest must incur, would work out at about three hundred dollars for each college year. That meant that what he could save in a year and a half of teaching would give him one year at college. Added to this was the fact that in the vacation – the two months of a teacher's vacation or the four months for a college vacation – he could work on a farm for his board and twenty dollars a month and save almost the whole of the twenty dollars. I have known at least one teacher, later on a leader of the medical profession of Alberta, who put in seven years of this life of teaching to get his college course. But in most cases there would be some extra source of supply: an uncle who owned a sawmill and could lend two or three hundred dollars, or an uncle over in the States, or an older brother who came down from the "shanties" in the spring with more money than he knew what to do with. For what could he do with it, except drink or go to college?

So in the end adversity was conquered, and the teachers passed through college and into law or medicine, with perhaps politics and public life, and added one more name to the roll of honour of men who "began as teachers." Some failed on the last lap, graduated, and then got married, tired of waiting for life to begin, and thus sank back again on teaching – as a high-school teacher, a better lot but still not good enough.

But the system was, and is, all wrong. Our teacher, with his thirty dollars a month, didn't get as much as our Old Tommy, the hired man, for he and his wife had twenty dollars a month and a cottage with it and a garden, milk and eggs and vegetables and meat to the extent of his end (I forget which) of any pig that was killed. A teacher situated like that could be a married man, as snug and respected as a Scottish dominie with his cottage and his kailyard, his trout rod and his half dozen Latin books bound in vellum – "as good as anybody," which is one of the things that a man has got to be in life if he is to live at all. The teachers weren't. I never was, and never felt I was, in the ten years I was a teacher. That is why later on I spent so many words in decrying schoolteaching as a profession, not seeing that schoolteaching is all right for those who are all right for it. The thing wrong is the setting we fail to give it.

Such was our school at School Section No. 3, Township of Georgina, County of York. It had also its amenities as well as its work. Now and again there were school "entertainments." I can't remember if the people paid to come. I rather think not, because in that case they wouldn't come. For an entertainment the school was lit with extra lamps. The teacher was chairman. The trustees made speeches or shook their heads and didn't. The trustees were among the old people who had come out from the "old country" with some part of another environment, something of an older world, still clinging to them. Some, especially Scotsmen like old Archie Riddell, would rise to the occasion and make a speech with quite a ring and a thrill to it, all about Marmion and Bruce and footprints on the sands of time. Then the teachers would say that we'd hear from Mr. Brown, and Mr. Brown, sitting in a sunken lump in a half-light, would be seen to shake his head, to assure us that we wouldn't. After which came violin music by local fiddlers, announced grandiloquently by the chairman as "Messrs. Park and Ego," although we knew that really they were just Henry Park and Angus Ego. Perhaps also some lawyer or such person from the village four miles away would drive up for the entertainment and give a reading or a recitation. It was under those circumstances that I first heard W. S. Gilbert's *Yarn of the "Nancy Bell."* It seemed to me wonderful beyond words, and the Sutton lawyer, a man out of wonderland.

But going to the country school just didn't work out. It was too far for us, and in rough weather and storm impossible, and it was out of the question for a younger section of the family (the ones in between the baby and ex-baby and the "big boys"). Moreover, my mother was haunted with the idea that if we kept on at the school we might sideslip and cease to be gentlemen. Already we were losing our Hampshire accent, as heard in *Twinkle, Twinkle, Little Star* – not "stah," and not "star," but something in between. I can still catch it if I am dead tired or delirious. We were beginning also to say "them there" and "these here," and "who all" and "most always," in short, phrases that no one can use and grow up a gentleman.

So my mother decided that she would teach us herself and with characteristic courage set herself at it, in the midst of all her other work with the baby and the little children and the kitchen and the servants and the house. Servants, of course, we always had: at least one maid – I beg pardon, I'm losing my language – I mean one "hired girl" and a "little girl" and generally an "old woman." Top wages were eight dollars a month; a little girl got five dollars. There was a certain queer gentility to it all. The hired man never sat down to eat with us, nor did the hired girl. Her status, in fact, as I see it in retrospect, was as low and humble as even an English earl could wish it. She just didn't count.

My mother had had in England a fine education of the Victorian finishing-school type and added to it a love and appreciation of literature that never left her all her life, not even

62   *Feast of Stephen*

at ninety years of age. So she got out a set of her old English schoolbooks that had come with us in a box from England – Colenso's *Arithmetic*, and Slater's *Chronology*, and Peter Parley's *Greece and Rome*, and Oldendorf's *New Method of French* – and gathered us around her each morning for school, opened with prayers, and needing them. But it was no good; we wouldn't pay attention, we knew it was only Mother. The books didn't work either – most of them were those English manuals of history and such, specially designed for ladies' schools and for ladies who had to teach their own children out in the "colonies." They were designed to get a maximum of effect for a minimum of effort, and hence they consisted mostly of questions and answers, the questions being what lawyers call leading questions, ones that suggest their own answers. Thus they reduced Roman history to something like this:

Q. Did not Julius Caesar invade Britain?

A. He did.

Q. Was it not in the year 55 B.C.?

A. It was.

Q. Was he not later on assassinated in Rome?

A. He was.

Q. Did not his friend Brutus take a part in assassinating him?

A. He did.

In this way one could take a birdlike flight over ancient history. I think we hit up about two hundred years every morning, and for ancient Egypt over one thousand years. I had such a phenomenal memory that it was all right for me, as I remembered the question and answer both. But my elder brothers Dick and Jim were of heavier academic clay, and so they just – as the politicians say – took it as read.

The *Arithmetic* of Bishop Colenso of Natal was heavier going. After multiplication and division it ran slap-bang into the Rule of Three, and Mother herself had never understood what the Rule of Three was, and if you went on beyond it all you found was practice and Aliquot Parts. I know now that all this is rule-of-thumb arithmetic, meant for people who can't reason it out, and brought straight down from the Middle Ages to Colenso. The glory of the unitary method, whereby if one man needs ten cigarettes a day then two men need twenty, and so on for as many men and as many cigarettes and as long a time as you like – this had not dawned on the British mind. I think it was presently imported from America.

So my mother's unhappy lessons broke down, and we were just about to be sent back to the red schoolhouse when by good luck we managed to secure a family tutor, from whom we received, for the next three of four years, teaching better than I have ever had since and better than any I ever gave in ten years as a schoolteacher. Our tutor was a young man off a near-by farm, stranded halfway through college by not having taught long enough and compelled to go back to teaching. So my grandfather from England put up the money (for fear, of course, that we might come back home on him), and there we were with a tutor and a schoolroom, inkwells, scribblers, slates — in fact, a whole academic outfit. Our tutor was known as "Harry Park" to his farm associates, but to us, at once and always, as "Mr. Park," and he ranked with Aristotle in dignity and width of learning. Never have I known anyone who better dignified his office, made more of it, so that our little schoolroom was as formal as Plato in his Academy could have wished it. Mr. Park rechristened my brother Jim as "James." to give him class, and Dick reappeared as "Arthur." The hours were as regular as the clock itself, in fact more so, since Mr. Park's watch soon took precedence over the kitchen clock, as the "classes" (made up of us four boys and my little sister, just qualified) were as neatly divided as in a normal school. I had to be Class I, but my brothers didn't care, as they freely admitted that I was the "cleverest" — they looked on it as no great asset. For certain purposes, poetry and history, we were all together.

For us "Mr. Park" knew everything, and I rather think that he thought this himself. Ask him anything and we got the answer. "Mr. Park, what were the Egyptians like?" He knew it and he told it, in measured formal language.

Under "Mr. Park's" teaching my brothers at least learned all that could be put into them, and I personally went forward like an arrow. At eleven years of age I could spell practically anything, knew all there was to know of simple grammar (syntax, parsing, analysis), beyond which there is nothing worth while anyway, knew Collier's *British History* and *History of English Literature*, all the geography of all the countries including Canada (the provinces of Canada which had not been in Mother's book), and in arithmetic had grasped the unitary system and all that goes with it and learned how to juggle with vulgar fractions even when piled up like a Chinese pagoda, and with decimals let them repeat as they would.

After Mr. Park came to us as tutor and the little red schoolhouse of School Section No. 3, Township of Georgina, was cut out, our isolation was all the more complete. We practically stayed on the farm. But of course a part of the old farm to children of eight to twelve years old, newly out from England, was a land of adventure; all the main part of it, as it sloped away to the south and west, was clear fields of the seven-acre pattern with snake fences all round it, piles of stones that had been cleared off the fields lying in the fence corners, raspberry bushes choking up the corners, but here and there an old elm tree springing up in an angle of the fence as a survival of the cleared forests. Elm trees have the peculiarity that they can do well alone, as no storm can break them, whereas hemlocks isolated by themselves are doomed. Hence the odd elm trees scattered all through this part of central Ontario, as if someone had set them on purpose to serve as shade trees or landscape decoration. Heaven knows no one did. For the earlier settlers, trees, to a great extent, were the enemy. The Upper Canada forest was slaughtered by the lumber companies without regard for the future, which in any case they could neither foresee nor control. In the early days the export of lumber was only in the form of square timber – great sticks of wood from twelve to eighteen inches each way, not cut up into the boards and deals and staves of the later lumber trade. Hence the trees were squared as they fell in the falling forest, and about one third of the main tree and all its branches burned up as litter to get rid of it. That was the early settler's idea of the bush: get rid of it where he could, and where it lay too low, too sunken, too marshy, to clear it. Then cut out the big trees and haul them out, leave the rest of the bushes there, and let farm clearings and roads get round it as best they could. As to planting any new trees to conserve the old ones, the farmers would have thought it a madman's dream. The only trees planted were the straight, fast-growing Lombardy poplars, still seen in their old age, set out in single or in little rows in front of the early Ontario houses. These owe their origin to the legend or the fact that they act as lightning conductors, a part of Benjamin Franklin's legacy to North America, along with the box stove and much else.

I am saying then that our old farm at its north end fell slap away down a steep hillside at the foot of which began the bush that spread off sideways in both directions as far as one could see and directly in front it rose again in a slope that blotted out all view of Lake Simcoe four miles away. Along the fringes of it were still some of the giant hemlocks that had escaped the full fury of the last bush fire, dead, charred, and still standing, but falling one by one. The bush, as one tried to penetrate it, grew denser and denser, mostly underbrush with tangled roots and second growth sprung up after the fires. It was so dense that for us it was impenetrable, and we ventured our way farther and farther in, carrying hatchets and alert for wildcats, which I am practically certain were not there and for bears, which had left years and years ago.

We had hardly any social life, as we were prevented, partly by "class" and mainly by distance, from going over to the other farms after dark. To one farm where lived a family of English children of something the same mixed antecedents as ourselves we sometimes went over for tea, and at times all the way to the village or to the lake-shore houses. But such treks meant staying overnight.

So mostly we stayed at home, and in the evenings we did our lessons, if we had lessons to do, and my mother read to us Walter Scott and carried us away to so deep an impression of the tournaments and battlefields of the Crusade and of the warring forests of Norman-Saxon England that any later "moving picture" of such things is but a mere blur of the surface. We cannot have it both ways. Intensity of mental impression and frequency of mental impression cannot go together. Robinson Crusoe's discovery of Friday's footprints on the sand – read aloud thus by candlelight to wondering children – has a dramatic "horror" to it (horror means making one's hair stand up) that no modern cinema or stage can emulate. Similarly I recall the reading aloud of *Tom Sawyer*, then, of course, still a new book, and the dramatic intensity of the disclosure that Indian Joe is sealed up in the great cave.

Our news from the outside world came solely in the form of the *Illustrated London News* sent out by my grandmother from England. In it we saw the pictures of the Zulu War and the (second) Afghan War and of Majuba Hill. With it we kept alive the British tradition that all Victorian children were brought up in, never doubting that of course the Zulus were wrong and the Afghans mistaken and the Boers entirely at fault. This especially, as Mother had lived in South Africa and said so.

On one point, however, of British Victorian orthodox faith I sideslipped at eight years old and have never entirely got back, and that too the greatest point in all British history. I refer to the question of George Washington and George the Third and whether the Americans had the right to set up a republic. It so happened that there came to our farm for a winter visit an English cousin of my father's who had become (I do not know how, for it must have been a rare thing in the seventies) a female doctor in Boston. She used to tell me, while Jim and Dick were mucking out the chores in the barnyard, which was their high privilege, about the United States and the Revolution, and when she saw how interested I was she sent to Boston and got a copy of Colonel Thomas Wentworth Higginson's *Young Folks'* (or *People's*) *History of the United States*. There it was, pictures and all – General Gage and the Boston Boys (very neat boys and a very neat general), Washington crossing the Delaware (hard going), Washington taking command at Cambridge. "Cousin Sophy" used to read it out loud to us – a needed rest for Walter Scott – and we were all fascinated with it, Jim and Dick with the pictures and the soldiers, but I chiefly from the new sense of the burning injustice of tyranny, a thing I had never got from history before.

Forthwith the theory of a republic, and the theory of equality, and the condemnation of hereditary rights seemed obvious and self-evident truths, as clear to me as they were to Thomas Jefferson. I stopped short at the queen partly, I suppose, because one touched there on heaven and hell and the church service and on ground which I didn't propose to tread. But for me, from then on, a hereditary lord didn't have a leg to stand on. In the sixty years (nearly seventy) since elapsed I have often tried to stand up hereditary peers again (I mean as members of a legislature), but they won't really stay up for me. I have studied it all, and lectured on it all, and written about it all. I know all about the British idea that if a thing has existed for a long time, and if most people like it and if it seems to work well and if it brings no sharp edge of cruelty and barbarity such as the world has learned again, then it is silly to break away from established institution on the ground of a purely theoretical fault. But I can't get by with the arguments. I broke with the House of Lords, with its hereditary peers and its bishops voting because they are bishops in 1879 – or whenever it was – and the breach has never been really healed. People from India have told me that no matter how scientific an education you may smear over an Indian doctor or scientist, put him in any emergency or danger and back he comes to his first beliefs: away goes medicine in favour of incantation and charms, and science abandons its instruments and its metric measurement and harks back a thousand years to astrology and mysticism.

I'm like that with my underlying Jeffersonian republicanism: back I slip to such crazy ideas as that all men are equal, and that hereditary rights (still saving out the British monrch) are hereditary wrongs.

Occasional treats broke the routine of our isolation on the farm, such as going into Sutton village for the "Twenty-fourth" (of May), the great annual holiday, or to see cricket matches between Sutton and other places, such as Newmarket, within cricket reach. For up to that time cricket still remained the game of the Upper Canada countryside, the game living on strongly against the competition of Yankee baseball and dying hard. At present cricket has shrunken in on Toronto and a few larger cities and school centres. But in the seventies and eighties it was everywhere. The wonder is, though, that it could survive at all – it makes such heavy demands – a decent "pitch" of prepared ground, without which the game is worthless, an outfield not too rough, and even for decent practice a certain minimum of players; while cricket "at the nets" is poor stuff without a good pitch and good bowling, especially if you haven't any nets. Nor can you have a real "match" at cricket without a real side of eleven or something close to it. Baseball, on the other hand, is quick and easy and universal. It can be played in a cow pasture or behind the barnyard or in the village street; two people can "knock out flies" and three can play at "rolling over the bat," and if you can't get nine for a game, a pitcher, catcher, and baseball will do – what's more, the game can be played out in an afternoon, an hour, or a minute. The wonder is that the British settlers in Upper Canada kept doggedly on with their British cricket as against the facile Yankee baseball and the indigenous lacrosse. I am quite sure that in the township of Georgina no one had ever seen the latter game in 1880.

Rarest and most striking of all treats was to be taken on a trip to Toronto on the new railway, which reached Lake Simcoe from the south by a branch line of the Toronto and Lake Nipissing Railway extended from Stouffville to Sutton and Jackson's Point Wharf (on the lake). It was part of that variegated network of little railways – of varied gauges and plans, all crooked as country roads, all afraid of a hill, and all trying to keep close to a steamer dock, each under different ownerships – which represents the shortsighted railway building of Ontario. Shortsighted? And yet I suppose it was hard to see ahead at all, in a community that stumbled and fell with every new onslaught of bad times and fought stubbornly against its forests and its torrents – half strangled in its own opportunity.

The completion of the railway and the arrival of the first train was a great event, much ringing of bells and blowing of whistles; then the train itself arrived by the sash factory and the gristmill. It made a great difference, too, with commodities, such as coal and oranges, seen in Sutton for the first time. But, as with most town and village advances of that date, it just went so far and then stopped. Sutton fell asleep again and woke only to the sound of the motor horn and the advent of the tourist, in another world years later.

But for us children a trip on the train to Toronto, a treat that was accorded to each of us about twice in the next three years, was a trip into wonderland – England had grown dim. Toronto, even the Toronto I describe in the next chapter, was marvellous beyond all description.

But the most real of our standing treats and holidays came to us on contact with Lake Simcoe. This grew out of our going to church every Sunday in summer to the Lake Shore Church four miles away. To our farm equipment there had been added a "phaeton" for Mother to drive and the kind of horse that is driven in a phaeton, which is born quiet, never grows old, and lives on into eternity. The ease and comfort of a phaeton can be appreciated by riding once in a buckboard (just once is all you need), a vehicle that means a set of slats on axles, with a seat on the slats. Its motion is similar to that of the new "seasickness medicine." A phaeton with steel springs, low entrance, and two seats can carry a capacity load and attain a speed, on the level, of six miles an hour. Even at that we walked in turns.

The parish church of Georgina stood on the high bank dotted with cedar trees overlooking Lake Simcoe, and oh! what a paradise the view presented. I have often and often and often written of Lake Simcoe. I know, with a few odd miles left out here and there, its every stick and stone, its island and points, and I claim that there is in all the world no more beautiful body of water. Writing it up years ago in a Canadian *Geographical Journal*, I said:

"The islands of the Aegean Sea have been regarded for centuries as a scene of great beauty; I know, from having seen them, that the Mediterranean coast of France and the valleys of the Pyrenees are a charm to the enchanted country;

and I believe that for those who like that kind of thing there is wild grandeur in the Highlands of Scotland, and a majestic solitude where the midnight sun flashes upon the ice peaks of Alaska. But to my thinking none of those will stand comparison with the smiling beauty of the waters, shores, and bays of Lake Simcoe and its sister lake, Couchiching. Here the blue of the deeper water rivals that of the Aegean; the sunlight flashes back in lighter colour from the sand bar on the shoals; the passing clouds of summer throw moving shadows as over a ripening field, and the mimic gales that play over the surface send curling caps of foam as white as ever broke under the bow of the Aegean galley.

"The Aegean is old. Its islands carry the crumbling temples of Homer's times. But everywhere its vegetation has been cut and trimmed and gardened by the hand of man. Simcoe is far older. Its forest outline is still what Champlain saw, even then unchanged for uncounted centuries. Look down through the clear water at the sunken trees that lie in the bay southeast of Sibbald's Point. They sank, as others sank before them, a hundred years ago; no hand of man has ever moved or touched them. The unquarried ledges of Georgina Island stood as they stand now when the Greeks hewed stone from the Pentelicus to build the Parthenon."

The whole point of our going to church on the lake shore on summer mornings was that we were allowed, by a special dispensation from the awful Sunday rules we were brought up on, to go in for a swim and to stick around beside the lake for an hour or so. The spot was one of great beauty. The earliest settlers had built a wooden church among the cedar trees, and in the very years of which I speak it was being replaced by the Lake Shore Church of cut stone that is one of the notable landmarks of the scenery of the district. It was built by the members of the Sibbald family, one of the chief families of the district, whose sons had gone abroad for service in the British Army and Navy and in India and, returning (in our day) as old men enriched in fortune and experience, built the stone church still standing as a memorial to their mother. A Latin motto (which outclassed me at nine years old) cut in a memorial stone on the face of the tower commemorates the fact. The church was built during two of our summers of churchgoing and swimming. The masons were not there on Sundays, but we could follow its progress every Sunday, in the stones new drilled for blasting, in the fresh-cut completed stones, and then in the rising layers of the walls, the upsweep of the tall roof (one Sunday to the next), the glass, the slates, and then – all of a sudden, as it were – we were singing in it.

Better still was it when my mother, a year or two later, 1880, was able to take a "summer cottage" near the church for a holiday of a month or so. "Summer cottage" is a courtesy title. It was an old log building built as a "parsonage," which in time proved unfit for habitation even by the meekest parson. But for a summer habitation it did well enough, and with it the glory of the lake and of the return to the water, which we lost since Porchester. We were like Viking children back to the sea! So will you find any British children, used to sight and sound of the sea, shut from the water a brief space in some inland or prairie town but exulting to get back to their agelong heritage. So were we with Lake Simcoe: making rafts of logs and boards before we had a boat, blown out to sea on our rafts and rescued, and thus learning what an offshore wind means – a thing that even today few Lake Ontario summer visitors understand. After rafts a flat-bottomed boat, liberally plugged up with hot pitch, then an attempt at making a sail and discovering that a flat-bottomed boat is no good – and so on, repeating the life of man on the ocean as the human race repeats in the individual its every stage of evolution.

In my case Lake Simcoe was a more interesting field of navigation then than now, more real. It is strange how our inland lakes have deteriorated from the navigation of reality to the navigation of luxury. What do you see now? Motorboats! Powerboats! Speed – sailing dinghies built like dishes and used for aquatic displays but with no connection with sailing in the real sense. And all this in any case only a fringe that fills the lakeshore resorts, crowds round luxury hotels, and leaves the open water of Simcoe and such lakes emptier than when La Salle crossed them.

Not so in the 1880s. Navigation filled the lake. Far out on its waters a long ribbon of smoke indicated a tug with a tow of logs heading for the mills at Jackson's Point. Sailing vessels, lumpy, heavy, and ungainly, and nearly as broad as long, carried quarry stone and heavy stuff from the top of Lake Couchiching to the railway pier at Belle Ewart. The *Emily May* steamer that circulated the lake all day and all night (in her prime days), with double crew, half of it awake and half asleep – two captains, two mates, two stewardesses, and two bartenders. The railways bit off her job point by point and place by place, the railway to Sutton and Jackson's

Point being the last straw that broke her back. Yet for years after the passenger boats in the real sense had gone the excursion lived on. *Ho! for Beaverton!* read its placards on the boardside fence, *Ho! for Jackson's Point* – and there it was on a summer morning carrying its sons of England, or its Knights of Ireland, its brass band, its improvised bar, its ladies' cabin as tight shut and as uncomfortable as being at home – all that went with Ho! for a day on the water in 1880. And so for years. Then came the motorcar and killed all that was left of navigation.

And all this time, although we didn't know, for my mother kept it hidden from us, at intervals my father drank, drove away to the village in the evening to return late at night after we were in bed, or lay round the farm too tired to work, and we thought it was the sun. And the more he drank, the more the farm slid sideways and downhill, and the more the cloud of debt, of unpaid bills, shadowed it over, and the deeper the shadow fell, the more he drank. My mother, I say, hid it all from us for years with a devotion that never faltered. My father, as he drank more, changed towards us from a superman and hero to a tyrant, from easy and kind to fits of brutality. I was small enough to escape from doing much of the farm chores and farm work. But I carry still the recollection of it – more, no doubt, than Jim or Dick ever did. In fact, the sight and memory of what domestic tyranny in an isolated, lonely home, beyond human help, can mean helped to set me all the more firmly in the doctrine of the rights of man and Jefferson's liberty.

By the end of the year 1881 the "old farm" as a going concern had pretty well come to a full stop. Bad farming had filled the fields with weeds; wild oats, a new curse of Ontario farming spread by the threshing machines, broke out in patches in the grain; low prices cut out all profit; apples rotted on the ground; potatoes hardly paid the digging. There was the interest on the mortgage of two hundred and fifty dollars a year, wages not paid, store bills not paid – just a welter of debt and confusion. So my father was led to give it all up and go away to Manitoba, the new land of promise that all the people on the farms were beginning to talk about. The opening of the Northwest by the Dominion taking it over had revealed the secret, so carefully guarded for two hundred years, that what had been thought of as a buffalo pasture and a fox range, a land for the trapper to share with the aurora borealis, was in reality a vast bed of deep alluvial soil, black mould two or three feet deep, the gift of the ages, the legacy of the grass and the flowers that had blossomed and withered unseen for centuries. You had but to scratch and throw in the wheat, and with that, such crops would grow as older Canada had never seen! But with that no clearing of the land to do, no stubborn fight against the stumps still all around us on the Ontario farms – empty country and land for the asking, one hundred and sixty acres free under the new homestead law and more if you wanted it "for a song." No phrase ever appealed to the farmer's heart like that of getting land for a song! In the glory of the vision he forgets that he can't sing and starts off looking for it.

To this was added the fact that there was rail connection now (1878) all the way to Manitoba by Chicago and St. Paul and the Red River route, and that it was known that the new government – which carried the election of 1878 under John A. Macdonald – was pledged to build a Canadian Pacific Railway clear across the plains and over the Rockies to the ocean. And with that was set up a sort of suction that began to draw people to Manitoba from all the Ontario farms, and presently beyond that from the old country itself, and in particular to Winnipeg, a place that had been a sort of straggled-out settlement of the Hudson's Bay Company, Fort Garry, and now broke on the horizon as a town whose geographical site in the bottleneck entrance of the West marked it as a future metropolis. Hence the "Winnipeg boom" and the noise of hammers and the saws, and the shouts of the real-estate agents, selling real estate all day and all night, and selling it so far out on the prairie that no one ever found it again.

My father was to go to Manitoba not on his own initiative – he hadn't any – but at the call of a younger brother who had gone ahead and was already riding on the crest of the wave. This was "my remarkable uncle," to whose memory I have devoted many sketches and even the scenario of a moving picture which I hope will one day move. He had come out to Canada, to our farm, in 1878, had captivated the countryside with his brilliant and unusual personality, taken a conspicuous part in the election of 1878, and passed on to the larger local notoriety in Toronto. He scented Winnipeg from afar, was one of the first in, and at the time of which I speak was piling up a fortune on paper, was elected to the New Manitoba legislature, and heaven knows what.

In my sketches I referred to my father and uncle as going away together, which is an error in the record. My father, and presently my brother Jim, followed.

So we had a sale at the farm at which, as I have said else-where, the lean cattle and the broken machinery fetched only about enough in notes of hand (nobody had cash) to pay for the whiskey consumed at the sale.

So my father left for the West, and my mother was left on the farm with the younger children and Old Tommy, and my elder brothers and I were sent away to school at Upper Canada College. That was for me practically the end of the old farm, though the rotten place hung round our family neck for years, unsalable. For the time being it was rented to the neighbouring farmer for two hundred and fifty dollars a year, the same amount as my mother had to pay on the mortgage. The farmer didn't pay the rent and Mother didn't pay the mortgage; all debts in those days dragged along like that. But the year after that my mother moved into Toronto on the strength of a casual legacy from England that should have been hoarded as capital but was burned up as income. Then my father came back (broke) from the Northwest in 1886, and that meant another move back from Toronto to the old farm, but I was not in it, being a boarder at Upper Canada College. Things went worse than ever for my father on his return to the farm – a shadowed, tragic family life into which I need not enter. I always feel that it is out of place in an autobiography to go into such details. The situation ended by my father leaving home again in 1887. No doubt he meant to come back, but he never did. I never saw him again. My mother lived on at the old farm, because it was unsalable, for four more years, with eight children to look after as best she could on about eighty dollars a month and with Old Tommy and his wife as bodyguard. Tommy's wages had not been paid for so long that he couldn't leave, but anyway he didn't want to. In his old-fashioned Yorkshire mind wages due from the aristocracy were like shares in the National Debt. My elder brothers Jim and Dick had both left home for good, both to the West, Dick into the Northwest Mounted Police and Jim in the wake of my remarkable uncle. That made me – my father being gone – the head of the family at seventeen. But since I was away at school and college and then teaching school, I was at the farm only on holidays and odd times. I at last got rid of the rotten old place on my mother's behalf simply by moving Mother off it and letting it go to the devil – mortgages, creditors, and all. I don't know who finally got it. But for me the old farm life ended with my going to Upper Canada College in the beginning of the year 1882.

The Mathematics
of the Lost Chord

Every one is familiar with the melodious yet melancholy song of "The Lost Chord." It tells us how, seated one day at the organ, weary, alone and sad, the player let his fingers roam idly over the keys, when suddenly, strangely, he "struck one chord which echoed like the sound of a Great Amen."

But he could never find it again. And ever since then there has gone up from myriad pianos the mournful laments for the Lost Chord. Ever since then, and this happened eighty years ago, wandering fingers search for the Lost Chord. No musician can ever find it.

But the trouble with musicians is that they are too dreamy, too unsystematic. Of course they could never find the Lost Chord by letting their fingers idly roam over the keys. What is needed is *method*, such as is used in mathematics every day. So where the musician fails let the mathematician try. He'll find it. It's only a matter of time.

The mathematician's method is perfectly simple – a matter of what he calls Permutations and Combinations – in other words, trying out all the Combinations till you get the right one.

He proposes to sound all the Combinations that there are, listen to them, and see which is the Great Amen. Of course a lot of combinations are not chords at all. They would agonize a musician. But the mathematician won't notice any difference. In fact the only one he would recognize is Amen itself, because it's the one when you leave church.

He first calculates how many chords he can strike in a given time. Allowing time for striking the chord, listening to it and letting it die away, he estimates that he can strike one every 15 seconds, or 4 to a minute, 240 to an hour. Working 7 hours a day with Sundays off and a half day off on Saturday, and a short vacation (at a summer school in Mathematics), he reaches the encouraging conclusion that *if need be* – if he didn't find the Chord sooner – he could sound as many as half a million chords within a single year!

The next question is how many combinations there are to strike. The mournful piano player would have sat strumming away for ever and never have thought that out. But it's not hard to calculate. A piano has 52 white notes and 36 black. The player can make a combination by striking 10 at a time (with all his fingers and thumbs), or any less number down to 2 at a time. Moreover he can, if a trained player, strike any 10 adjacent or distant. Even if he has to strike notes at the extreme left and in the middle and at the extreme right all in the same combination, he does it by rapidly sweeping his left hand towards the right, or his right towards the left. There is a minute fraction between the initial strokes of certain notes, but not enough to prevent them sounding together as a combination.

This makes the calculation simplicity itself. It merely means calculating the total combinations of 88 things, taken 2 at a time, 3 at a time and so on up to 10 at a time.

The combinations, 2 notes at a time

Are $\dfrac{88 \times 87}{1 \times 2}$ 3,828

For 3 at a time $\dfrac{88 \times 87 \times 86}{1 \times 2 \times 3}$ 109,736

For 4 at a time $\dfrac{88 \times 87 \times 86 \times 85}{1 \times 2 \times 3 \times 4}$ 2,331,890

For 5 at a time $\dfrac{88 \times 87 \times 86 \times 85 \times 84}{1 \times 2 \times 3 \times 4 \times 5}$ 39,175,750

For 6 at a time $\dfrac{88 \times 87 \times 86 \times 85 \times 84 \times 83}{1 \times 2 \times 3 \times 4 \times 5 \times 6}$ 541,931,236

For 7 at a time $\dfrac{88 \times 87 \times 86 \times 85 \times 84 \times 83 \times 82}{1 \times 2 \times 3 \times 4 \times 5 \times 6 \times 7}$ 6,348,337,336

For 8 at a time $\dfrac{88 \times 87 \times 86 \times 85 \times 84 \times 83 \times 82 \times 81}{1 \times 2 \times 3 \times 4 \times 5 \times 6 \times 7 \times 8}$ 64,276,915,527

For 9 at a time $\dfrac{88 \times 87 \times 86 \times 85 \times 84 \times 83 \times 82 \times 81 \times 80}{1 \times 2 \times 3 \times 4 \times 5 \times 6 \times 7 \times 8 \times 9}$ 571,350,360,240

For 10 at a time $\dfrac{88 \times 87 \times 86 \times 85 \times 84 \times 83 \times 82 \times 81 \times 80 \times 79}{1 \times 2 \times 3 \times 4 \times 5 \times 6 \times 7 \times 8 \times 9 \times 10}$ ... 4,513,667,845,896

For all combinations 5,156,227,011,439

This gives us then an honest straightforward basis on which to start the search. The player setting out at his conscientious pace of half a million a year has the consoling

Feast of Stephen

feeling that he may find the Great Amen first shot, and at any rate he's certain to find it in 10,000,000 years.

It's a pity that the disconsolate players were so easily discouraged. The song was only written eighty years ago; they've hardly begun. Keep on, boys.

Hoodoo McFiggin's Christmas

This Santa Claus business is played out. It's a sneaking, underhand method, and the sooner it's exposed the better.

For a parent to get up under cover of the darkness of night and palm off a ten-cent necktie on a boy who had been expecting a ten-dollar watch, and then say that an angel sent it to him, is low, undeniably low.

I had a good opportunity of observing how the thing worked this Christmas, in the case of young Hoodoo McFiggin, the son and heir of the McFiggins, at whose house I board.

Hoodoo McFiggin is a good boy – a religious boy. He had been given to understand that Santa Claus would bring nothing to his father and mother because grown-up people don't get presents from the angels. So he saved up all his pocket-money and bought a box of cigars for his father and a seventy-five-cent diamond brooch for his mother. His own fortunes he left in the hands of the angels. But he prayed. He prayed every night for weeks that Santa Claus would bring him a pair of skates and a puppy-dog and an air-gun and a bicycle and a Noah's ark and a sleigh and a drum – altogether about a hundred and fifty dollars' worth of stuff.

I went into Hoodoo's room quite early Christmas morning. I had an idea that the scene would be interesting. I woke him up and he sat up in bed, his eyes glistening with radiant expectation, and began hauling things out of his stocking.

The first parcel was bulky; it was done up quite loosely and had an odd look generally.

"Ha! Ha!" Hoodoo cried gleefully, as he began undoing it. "I'll bet it's the puppy-dog, all wrapped up in paper!"

And was it the puppy-dog? No, by no means. It was a pair of nice strong, number-four boots, laces and all, labelled, "Hoodoo, from Santa Claus," and underneath Santa Claus had written, "95 net."

The boy's jaw fell with delight. "It's boots," he said, and plunged in his hand again.

He began hauling away at another parcel with renewed hope on his face.

This time the thing seemed like a little round box. Hoodoo tore the paper off it with a feverish hand. He shook it; something rattled inside.

"It's a watch and chain! It's a watch and chain!" he shouted. Then he pulled the lid off.

And was it a watch and chain? No. It was a box of nice, brand-new celluloid collars, a dozen of them all alike and all his own size.

The boy was so pleased that you could see his face crack up with pleasure.

He waited a few minutes until his intense joy subsided. Then he tried again.

This time the packet was long and hard. It resisted the touch and had a sort of funnel shape.

"It's a toy pistol!" said the boy, trembling with excitement. "Gee! I hope there are lots of caps with it! I'll fire some off now and wake up father."

No, my poor child, you will not wake your father with that. It is a useful thing, but it needs not caps and it fires no bullets, and you cannot wake a sleeping man with a toothbrush. Yes, it was a tooth-brush – a regular beauty, pure bone all through, and ticketed with a little paper, "Hoodoo, from Santa Claus."

Again the expression of intense joy passed over the boy's face, and the tears of gratitude started from his eyes. He wiped them away with his tooth-brush and passed on.

The next packet was much larger and evidently contained something soft and bulky. It had been too long to go into the stocking and was tied outside.

"I wonder what this is," Hoodoo mused, half afraid to open it. Then his heart gave a great leap, and he forgot all his other presents in the anticipation of this one. "It's the drum, all wrapped up!"

Drum nothing! It was pants – a pair of the nicest little short pants – yellowish-brown short pants – with dear little stripes of colour running across both ways, and here again Santa Claus had written, "Hoodoo, from Santa Claus, one fort net."

But there was something wrapped up in it. Oh yes! There was a pair of braces wrapped up in it, braces with a little steel sliding thing so that you could slide your pants up to your neck, if you wanted to.

The boy gave a dry sob of satisfaction. Then he took out

his last present. "It's a book," he said, as he unwrapped it. "I wonder if it is fairy stories or adventures. Oh, I hope it's adventures! I'll read it all morning."

No, Hoodoo, it was not precisely adventures. It was a small family Bible. Hoodoo had now seen all his presents, and he arose and dressed. But he still had the fun of playing with his toys. That is always the chief delight of Christmas morning.

First he played with his tooth-brush. He got a whole lot of water and brushed all his teeth with it. This was huge.

Then he played with his collars. He had no end of fun with them, taking them all out one by one and swearing at them, and then putting them back and swearing at the whole lot together.

The next toy was his pants. He had immense fun there, putting them on and taking them off again, and then trying to guess which side was which by merely looking at them.

After that he took his book and read some adventures called "Genesis" till breakfast-time.

Then he went downstairs and kissed his father and mother. His father was smoking a cigar, and his mother had her new brooch on. Hoodoo's face was thoughtful, and a light seemed to have broken in upon his mind. Indeed, I think it altogether likely that next Christmas he will hang on to his own money and take chances on what the angels bring.

Feast of Stephen

The Hero of Home Week

How Ed Smith Came Back to Our Home Town

Last week was Old Home Week in the town which I happen to inhabit in the summer. They put it over on a pretty big scale, so as to make a success of it. The town had made a big hit with Mother's Day just a little before, and with Father's Day the week after that, and, I believe, there was talk already of a Grandfather's Afternoon. So, naturally, the committee wanted Home Week to go over well.

They had the town decorated and all that sort of thing: flags across the main street, American, British, Belgian, Japanese and French – a lot they had left over from the war time – and they had a band in the park for an hour every evening, and something going on all the time. The stores, too, kept wide open so as to make it feel like a holiday.

There were, I understand, a great many who came back to the town for Old Home Week: some who were on the road and generally came home for week-ends, and others who didn't "make it" more than once a month or so, and others again who had been away for a year, or maybe for two years straight.

But the most noticeable one of the returning sons of the town was Ed Smith, who hadn't been back home for ten years on end, and hadn't even seen the place in all that time. Ed had wired from Saskatoon, Saskatchewan, "Hope to make town for Old Home Week," and the local papers, both of them, had carried headlines: "Will Make Town for Old Home Week – Ed Smith Will Hit the Home Trail from Saskatoon, Sask."

There was talk of a demonstration at the train for Ed. But the boys were mostly in the stores and couldn't make it. The committee meant to go down in a body and welcome Ed, but none of them were able to get off. However, Ed got a hack at the station and drove to the hotel by himself. He told us that it was the same old hack that he had driven away in ten years ago, and the same driver, too. He said the station looked just about the same, too, the track just where it was, and the platform and everything.

The committee had got up a special luncheon for Ed, that is to say, they all had dinner at the Continental Hotel at noon. (It was quicker than going home. They generally ate dinner there.) And I was present as a sort of guest, with the right to pay for my dinner. As a result, we all ate there and each paid for his own dinner, and Ed sat with us and paid for his. But, of course, Ed was the hero of the occasion and naturally as the dinner got near its end the talk fell on old times, and Ed lit a cigar and began to talk of what he remembered.

"I remember," he said, "that years ago (most of you fellows wouldn't remember it) there was a little old frame store down on the corner of West Street – queer-looking, tumble-down place – it's a pity these little old joints get knocked down–"

"It's not knocked down," said one of the listeners. "It's right there."

"Oh, is it?" said Ed. "Well, as I was saying, there used to be a queer old character living in it, called Mulvaney, a real old-timer – you fellows wouldn't remember him–"

"Oh, yes, yes," interrupted three or four of the men, "he's there still. That's right. Jim Mulvaney's still on the corner of West Street."

"Is he?" Ed said, and he looked for the moment a little set back. "Well, what I was going to say was that in the days I'm speaking of Mulvaney had a dog, the queerest-looking creature you ever saw. It was all brown, except just one ear and that was all white–"

"He's got it still," chorused the crowd all together. "Jim Mulvaney has that dog yet–"

"Has he? What?" said Ed, evidently a little discouraged. "He has, eh? Well, I'm surprised. I was going to tell you about a darned funny thing that happened one day with that dog when I used to live here. Old Jim used to like to sit out in front of the house on the step with the dog beside him and watch the people go by. And a queer thing about that dog was he never could stand the sight of anything blood-red, just like what they say about a bull. Well, the Chief of Police happened to come along, and as it was a pretty warm evening, darned if he didn't happen to stop right there and pull out a big red handkerchief and mop his face with it. Well, sir," continued Ed, beginning to laugh, "as soon as the dog saw this, darned if he didn't make one leap for the Chief—"

But this time Ed couldn't even finish his sentence.

"He bit him again yesterday," they all interrupted.

"He did!" said Ed. "Well's that's a caution. But I was going to say this time that I remember he leaped at him from behind, and, say, you'd have laughed to see it, he bit the seat right out of his pants!!"

"So he did yesterday!" cried all the listeners in a chorus.

That quieted Ed down for a little. But naturally after a while he got talking again, speaking of this person and that that he remembered from the old days.

"Poor old Tim Jackson," he said, "some of you may remember him. He lived in the little cottage with all the flowers in front of it along Centre Street. Poor Tim, he had T.B. pretty bad." (Ed lowered his voice to a becoming tone.) "I guess he didn't last much longer. They said he'd die that winter."

"No," somebody said quietly. "Tim's not dead. He's there still."

"He's got over his T.B.?" Ed said.

"No, he has it still."

"Is that so?" said Ed. "Well, anyway, they said he wouldn't last through that winter."

"They say he'll hardly last this," somebody said.

There was a little silence for a while. Then Ed began again. But this time, instead of telling stories, he asked questions.

"What became of old Gillespie that had the lumber yard?" he asked.

"He's got it still," they said.

"Oh, has he? And where's old man Samson that kept the hotel down beyond the station?"

"He's there. He's keeping it now."

"And who's got Ed Bailey's pool room now?"

"Ed has."

"Is that so? I remember there used to be an old Swede who used to be the marker at the pool room and sell the cigars – old Heiney, they used to call him – a darned decent old feller. I'd give five dollars to see old Heiney again."

"I think he's outside," said one of the listeners. "I'm sure I saw him as we came in through the lobby. Wait a minute and I'll see if he's there."

"That's all right," Ed said. "I'll see him later."

After that Ed stopped asking about the people he used to

know, and he began instead telling about how he left the town and what happened to him.

"I had it pretty hard for a while," said Ed, lighting a fresh cigar and sitting well back in his chair as he warmed to his narration. "When I left here I was stone broke and I thought I'd head west and try what I could do. I hit Winnipeg one dark winter morning to find myself absolutely alone and without a cent. . . ."

"Say, excuse me, Eddie," said one of the boys. "I guess I'll have to be getting back to the store."

"That's all right, Jim," said Ed, and as Jim left he continued, "Well, I thought I'd look around and see where I could borrow five dollars–"

"Say, I guess I'll have to be going, too," said another of the boys, looking at his watch. "You'll excuse me, won't you, Ed?"

"Certainly," said Eddie, "that's all right, Alf. Well, I remembered a fellow I used to know in Toronto and I managed to find him and he lent me five, and I got on a train and beat it as far as Brandon to work on a farm. At first it was tough–"

"I'll say it was!" said one of the listeners. "But, say, Ed, I'll see you later on, eh? I'll have to go."

"That's all right," Ed said. "At first it was tough–"

"I guess I'd better go along with Harry," said another of the crowd, "so I won't have to interrupt you any further. So long, Ed."

"So long, Will," said Ed. "At first it was tough–"

"Hold on a second, Ed," said another man. "I don't believe I'd better stay either. My time is just about out. Did any of the fellers pay for you, Ed?"

"That's all right," Ed said.

When this man had gone, Eddie and I were alone and I let him finish telling me how tough it was to find himself in a place where he had no friends. I thought I could guess it anyway.

After he had finished his reminiscences, Ed rose up. "Let's take a whirl along the street," he suggested. "I'd like to look in and see one or two of the old boys. Here's Mel Rose's hat store. I must drop in on old Mel. I'll bet he'll be surprised."

We dropped in. The store was full of people. "Mr. Rose in?" asked Ed of one of the shop men. "He's up in the middle of the store," the man said.

Mel Rose was standing with a customer, selling a hat. He saw Ed and turned his head slightly. "How are you, Mr.

Smith, something in a summer hat? Miss Williams, something in a summer hat, please!"

Just that. As if Ed had only been away a day. He meant no harm. The years is just a day in our town.

We left the store and went into the jeweler's next door to it. Ed said he wanted badly to see Frank Padden, the jeweler, one of his oldest pals around the town. His idea was that he'd drop in and give Frank the surprise of his life.

Frank shook hands limply over the counter. "How are you, Ed?" he said. "Something in a watch?"

In the next store Ed's old friend, Pete Williams, said, "Something in a necktie?" and in the store beyond that, Joe Kay, one of the best fellers (so Ed had assured me) that ever breathed, shook hands and queried, "Anything in summer shirting, Ed?"

But that time Ed was about all finished. The sunshine of the old town was fading out for him. He should have understood, but he didn't.

"I guess I'll go into the bank and get some money," he murmured. I knew what he meant. He was going to leave town.

We went into the bank and Ed wrote a check for fifteen dollars. The clerk looked at it. "I'll have to show it to the manager," he said.

"Tell him Mr. Ed Smith, that used to live here," said Ed.

The manager came out of his little office with the check in his hand. He saw Ed.

"You remember me, Mr. Calson," said Ed, shaking hands. "I used to live here."

"Oh, yes," the manager said in a dubious way. "I remember you, but I was just looking at the check. I suppose it's all right, eh! There's ten cents exchange," he called to the teller. "Well, good afternoon."

We left the bank.

"There used to be a four-ten train for the city," said Ed humbly.

"There still is," I answered.

He took it.

For him, the next time the banners of Old Home Week will float in vain.

But Ed was wrong. He had made a mistake. The old town had given him the best welcome of all. The welcome of familiarity. And he had not seen it.

Mr. Chairman,
I Beg to Move—

*Showing the Wonderful Effectiveness of What Is Called
Legislative Procedure*

"There is no doubt," says one of the recent Outlines of the
Sidelines of History, "that the adoption of legislative procedure marked a great forward step in the progress of
government. It lent to debate an order and precision before
unknown; it clarified thought, and restrained the turbulence
of argument by the dignity of formal address."

Quite so. But did it? Let us see how it has worked out in
some of the Meetings.

I

The Man Who Started the Trouble: A.D. 1295

Scene: Ye Chapel of St. Stephen's in Ye Borough of West
Minster.

Ye Speaker: An it please ye, my good Knights and Bur-
gesses, sith this is a regular or model Parliament it would
seem good to me that we frame or – as who should say –
draught a set of rules whereby our parlement or, so to speak,
our debate, shall be guided: Such as, first or in primis, that
none shall speak when I am talking; second, that when
others speak all shall be in order and form, such that not
twenty speak at once as hitherto, but only one, or, so to
speak, solus–

Fascinated with the idea, the houses of the King's parliament of Edward I got together and made a set of rules of
which the awful consequences are still among us. As
witness–

II

*The Familiar Scene When the Ladies' Three-Weekly
Discussion Club Undertakes Its Annual
Discussion of the Club's Finances.
Verbatim Report:*

86

Mrs. A.: I'd like to rise—

The Chairman-woman: I don't believe you can.

Mrs. A: But I am—

The Chair: I mean, I don't think you're in order. There's an amendment to the previous motion still, I think, before us.

Mrs. B: If you mean my amendment, I had something that I want to add to it anyway, but I don't mind leaving it over if Jennie feels—

The Chair (pounding on the table with a mallet): You're out of order.

Mrs. B: I only want to say—

The Chair: You can't. There's a motion still before us and an amendment.

Mrs. C.: But can't she withdraw her amendment? I'd like to move that Mrs. B—

The Chair: You've heard the motion, ladies? Or no, I beg your pardon, it hasn't been seconded. Doesn't anybody second it?

Mrs. D: Before you take up that, wouldn't it perhaps be better—

Mrs. A, B, C, and half the alphabet: Order!

Mrs. D: I'm not—

The Alphabet: You are!

The Chair (pounding): Ladies! Ladies!

Mrs. X: I'd like to second the motion, only I'd want to say at the same time that I think that Nellie—

Mrs. Q: Don't you think, Madame Chairman, that we've done enough for one morning? I'm afraid lunch will be utterly overdone if we keep on. I told them one o'clock in the kitchen.

The Chair: Will you move a motion to adjourn?

Mrs. Q: Yes, if it is necessary. All I mean is that lunch—

And so after a hard morning they at last get adjourned.

III

*How the Committee of Professors Undertake to
Bring in a Report to the Faculty*

The Chairman: Now, gentlemen, you have heard the remit, that this committee is to report on the question of the use of lead pencils in place of pen and ink.

Professor A: Mr. Chairman, I should like to ask a question, if I may.

The Chair: I don't believe you can. You see, for the moment there is no business before us, and until we have some definite corpus loquendi as a prima materies there is nothing on which a question could depend.

Professor A: May I perhaps submit a motion?

The Chair (looking in a book of rules and shaking his head): I don't think a motion would lie. It has nothing to lie on.

Professor B: I think, Mr. Chairman, that a motion that the remit be remitted would lie. Then I think Professor A could move for leave to ask a question as arising out of the remit.

Professor C: I don't want to delay the work of the committee, but I cannot agree with Professor B. I do not think that any motion can lie at all until the chair sua sponte, or to put it more simply still, ab origine voluntaria, submits the remit to the committee. Till that is done the remit itself is in vacuo.

(General murmurs of approval. Professor C has evidently hit out a home-run. And so by careful legislative procedure, crawling forward from cover to cover, they manage to get to Professor A's question.)

The Chair: I think, then, Professor A, that we may now hear your question.

Professor A: What I wish to ask, Mr. Chairman, is the precise sense in which the committee is to understand the word "lead pencil"; or rather, to be more exact, the sense to be attached to the term "lead." The word "pencil," I think, we may accept as a term generally understood. But the word "lead" offers difficulties. Does the remit include colored leads or only black; would this change permit the use of crayons, chalks and indelible pencils? In other words, I think we must formulate a definition of the word "lead."

The Chair: I think Professor A's remarks are entirely to the point. – Ha! Ha! Gentlemen, you must pardon me, I hadn't intended any witticism – to the point, ha! ha!

All the Committee: Ha! Ha! To the point – ha! ha!

The Chairman (wiping his streaming eyes): Order, gentlemen, order. (And when the laughter has all died down). Well, then, we must define the word "lead." Has anybody an encyclopedia here?

Professor C: Yes, I have one in my pocket.

The Chair: Will some one move that Professor C read what it says about it?

Feast of Stephen

General murmur: Carried.

Professor C: Lead. A mineral carboniferous substance generally found in oleaginous rock. Lead was known to the ancients and was probably (but you can't bet on it) the plumbum of the Romans: whence the word plumb, meaning heavy or straight as in "plumb" line; the word must be distinguished from "plumb," meaning a fruit (Sanskrit, plupp), which originated in Corinth, which was famous for its fruit trees, a growth due no doubt to the favorable breezes from the Aegean, which was perhaps so called from its "Aege" or border as seen in Aegis, the shield carried by the Roman foot-soldier, but carefully to be distinguished from the pelta or shield of the Greek hoplite. The Greeks, in fact, were a great people–

Professor X (aged 79, waking up): I think, Mr. Chairman, that our meeting has been sufficiently protracted, and as I think I heard the dormitory dinner-bell–

The Chair: Shall we then defer progress and adjourn till this day six months–

All: Carried!

IV

The Crude Proceedings of Those Who Never Heard of the Model Parliament of Edward I

The scene is laid in any board-room where the directors of any great industrial company are making a simple little arrangement not involving more than fifty or sixty million dollars.

The Chairman: Well, then, what we want to do is to split the shares two for one. That's it, isn't it?

Murmurs of "Agreed."

The Chairman: To take 100 millions of the new stock, the holders to take up at par–

Murmurs of "Agreed."

The Chairman (to some one): Will you get that drafted, and will you see about the legislative authorization (they know all about it) – and – that was the only thing this morning, wasn't it? All right, then we'll adjourn till next time, eh?

Love me,
Love my Letters

The Use of Ink for the First Inklings of Love

There is a proverb which says a man is known by the company he keeps. There is a saying also that a man is best known by the song he sings. It is claimed, too, that people can always be distinguished by the books that they read, and by the pictures that they admire, and by the clothes that they wear.

All this may be true. But, to my thinking, the truest test of character is found in the love letters that people write. Each different type of man or woman – including girls – has his, or her, perhaps their, own particular way of writing love letters.

As witness to which, let me submit to the reader's judgment a carefully selected set of love letters present and past. I need hardly say that the letters are not imaginary, but that each of them is an actual sample taken right out of the post office – no, I don't think I need to say it.

I

The Old-fashioned Style

Love letter of the year 1828 sent by messenger from Mr. Ardent Heartful, The Hall, Notts, England, to Miss Angela Blushanburn, The Shrubberies, Hops, Potts, Shrops, England, begging her acceptance of a fish:

"Respected Miss Angela:

"With the consent of your honored father and your esteemed mother, I venture to send to you by the messenger who bears you this, a fish. It has, my respected Miss Angela, for some time been my most ardent desire that I might have the good fortune to present to you as the fruit of my own endeavours, a fish. It was this morning my good fortune to land while angling in the stream that traverses your property, with the consent of your father, a fish.

"In presenting for your consumption, with your parents' consent, respected Miss Angela, this fish, may I say that the fate of this fish which will thus have the inestimable privilege

90

of languishing upon your table conveys nothing but envy to one who, while what he feels cannot be spoken, still feels as deeply as should feel, if it does feel, this fish.

"With the expression of a perfect esteem for your father and mother, believe me,

Your devoted,
"Ardent Heartful."

II

The Newer Style of To-day

Love letter composed by Professor Albertus Dignus, senior professor of English rhetoric and diction at the University, and famous as the most brilliant essayist outside of the staff of the *London Times,* to Miss Maisie Beatit of the chorus of the Follies-in-Transit company at Memphis, Tenn.:

"Cuckoo! my little peacherino, and how is she to-night? I wish she was right here, yum! yum! I got her tootsie weenie letter this morning. I hustled to the post office so fast to get it I nearly broke my slats. And so it really longs for me, does she? and did you really mean it? Well, you certainly look like a piece of chocolate to me! In fact, you're some bird! You're my baby all right," – and so forth for three pages. After which, the professor turns back to work on his essay – "The Deterioration of the English Language Among the Colored Races of Africa."

III

Truly Rural

Passionate Love Letter from Mr. Ephraim Cloverseed, Arcadia Post Office, Vermont, to Miss Nettie Singer, also of Arcadia, but at present on the cash in the Home Restaurant, 7860 Sixth Avenue, New York:

"Dear Nettie:

"There was a sharp frost last night which may do considerable harm to the fall wheat. Till last Tuesday there had not been no frost that you wouldn't have noticed any. Some think we are in for a hard winter. Some think if it clears off a bit between this and New Year's it may not be but some don't. I seen a couple of crows in the pasture yesterday but you can't always bank on that. I've been troubled again with my toe. But my rheumatism seems a whole lot better from that last stuff. My left leg has been pretty stiff again but the liniment has done my right arm good. Well, I will now close,

"Ephraim."

IV

Hydraulic Love

Letter from Mr. Harry P. Smith, hydraulic engineer and surveyor, writing to Miss Georgia Sims, from Red Gulch Creek in the wilds of New Ontario. Everybody knows that Harry has been just crazy over Georgia for three years.

"Dear Georgia:

"We got in here through the bush yesterday and it certainly is a heck of a place to try to run a sight line in. The rock is mostly basaltic trap, but there are faults in it here and there that have been filled with alluvial deposit. It would be pretty hard to give you an estimate of the probable mineral content. But I should say you would have a fair chance of striking gas here if you went deep enough. But your overhead would be a whopper. Well, Georgia, I must now close.

"Harry."

The Answers They Got

The answer received by Mr. Ardent Heartful, Anno Domini, 1828:

"Sir Joshua and Lady Blushanburn present their compliments to Mr. Ardent Heartful and desire to thank him for the fish which Mr. Heartful has had the kindness to forward to their daughter and which they have greatly enjoyed. Sir Joshua and Lady Blushanburn will be pleased if Mr. Heartful will present himself in person for such further conversation in regard to this fish as connects it with his future intentions."

What the Professor Got

The answer from Miss Maisie Beatit of the Follies-in-Transit Company, Memphis, Tenn.:

"My dear Professor:

"It was with the most agreeable feelings of gratification that I received your letter this morning.

"The sentiments which you express and the very evident manifestation thus conveyed of your affection towards myself fill me, sir, with the most lively satisfaction. . . ." After which Maisie got tired of copying word after word of the Complete Letter-Writer and so she just added in her own style,

"Ain't you the Kidder? Our next jump is Kansas City.

"Maisie."

Womanly Epistle Sent from Postal Station B-28,
New York, to Arcadia, P.O., Vermont

"Dear Ephraim:

"I was glad to get your letter. I was sorry to hear there has been so much frost. I was glad to hear there are still crows in the bush. I was sorry to hear your toe is no better. I was glad to hear your rheumatism is some better. I am glad your leg is nicely. I must now close.

"Nettie."

The Answer from Miss Georgia Sims, Bloor Street, Toronto

She didn't answer.

Little query for the reader just at the end. Which of these various couples will get married first and stay married longest. Quite right. You guessed it immediately. There's no doubt about it, to persons of judgment in such things.

Saloonio

A Study in Shakespearean Criticism

They say that young men fresh from college are pretty posi-
tive about what they know. But from my own experience of
life, I should say that if you take a comfortable, elderly man
who hasn't been near a college for about twenty years, who
has been pretty liberally fed and dined ever since, who
measures about fifty inches around the circumference, and
has a complexion like a cranberry by candlelight, you will
find that there is a degree of absolute certainty about what he
thinks he knows that will put any young man to shame. I
am specially convinced of this from the case of my friend
Colonel Hogshead, a portly, choleric gentleman who made a
fortune in the cattle-trade out in Wyoming, and who, in his
later days, has acquired a chronic idea that the plays of
Shakespeare are the one subject upon which he is most qualified to speak personally.

He came across me the other evening as I was sitting by
the fire in the club sitting-room looking over the leaves of
The Merchant of Venice, and began to hold forth to me
about the book.

"*Merchant of Venice*, eh? There's a play for you, sir! There's
genius! Wonderful, sir, wonderful! You take the characters
in that play and where will you find anything like them?
You take Antonio, take Sherlock, take Saloonio–"

"Saloonio, Colonel?" I interposed mildly, "aren't you making a mistake? There's a Bassanio and a Salanio in the play,
but I don't think there's any Saloonio, is there?"

For a moment Colonel Hogshead's eye became misty with
doubt, but he was not the man to admit himself in error:

"Tut, tut! young man," he said with a frown, "don't skim
through your books in that way. No Saloonio? Why, of
course there's a Saloonio!"

"But I tell you, Colonel," I rejoined, "I've just been reading
the play and studying it, and I know there's no such character–"

"Nonsense, sir, nonsense!" said the Colonel, "why he comes
in all through; don't tell me, young man, I've read that play

myself. Yes, and seen it played, too, out in Wyoming, before you were born, by fellers, sir, that could act. No Saloonio, indeed! why, who is it that is Antonio's friend all through and won't leave him when Bassoonio turns against him? Who rescues Clarissa from Sherlock, and steals the casket of flesh from the Prince of Aragon? Who shouts at the Prince of Morocco, 'Out, out, you damned candlestick?' Who loads up the jury in the trial scene and fixes the doge? No Saloonio! By gad! in my opinion, he's the most important character in the play—"

"Colonel Hogshead," I said very firmly, "there isn't any Saloonio and you know it."

But the old man had got fairly started on whatever dim recollection had given birth to Saloonio; the character seemed to grow more and more luminous in the Colonel's mind, and he continued with increasing animation:

"I'll just tell you what Saloonio is: he's a type. Shakespeare means him to embody the type of the perfect Italian gentleman. He's an idea, that's what he is, he's a symbol, he's a unit—"

Meanwhile I had been searching among the leaves of the play. "Look here," I said, "here's the list of the Dramatis Personæ. There's no Saloonio there."

But this didn't dismay the Colonel one atom. "Why, of course there isn't," he said. "You don't suppose you'd find Saloonio there! That's the whole art of it! That's Shakespeare! That's the whole gist of it! He's kept clean out of the Personæ – gives him scope, gives him a free hand, makes him more of a type than ever. Oh, it's a subtle thing, sir, the dramatic art!" continued the Colonel, subsiding into quiet reflection; "it takes a feller quite a time to get right into Shakespeare's mind and see what he's at all the time."

I began to see that there was no use in arguing any further with the old man. I left him with the idea that the lapse of a little time would soften his views on Saloonio. But I had not reckoned on the way in which old men hang on to a thing. Colonel Hogshead quite took up Saloonio. From that time on Saloonio became the theme of his constant conversation. He was never tired of discussing the character of Saloonio, the wonderful art of the dramatist in creating him, Saloonio's relation to modern life, Saloonio's attitude toward women, the ethical significance of Saloonio, Saloonio as compared with Hamlet, Hamlet as compared with Saloonio – and so on, endlessly. And the more he looked into Saloonio, the more he saw in him.

Saloonio seemed inexhaustible. There were new sides to him – new phases at every turn. The Colonel even read over the play, and finding no mention of Saloonio's name in it, he swore that the books were not the same books they had had out in Wyoming; that the whole part had been cut clean out to suit the book to the infernal public schools, Saloonio's language being – at any rate, as the Colonel quoted it – undoubtedly a trifle free. Then the Colonel took to annotating his book at the side with such remarks as, "Enter Saloonio," or "A tucket sounds; enter Saloonio, on the arm of the Prince of Morocco." When there was no reasonable excuse for bringing Saloonio on the stage the Colonel swore that he was concealed behind the arras, or feasting within with the doge.

But he got satisfaction at last. He had found that there was nobody in our part of the country who knew how to put a play of Shakespeare on the stage, and took a trip to New York to see Sir Henry Irving and Miss Terry do the play. The Colonel sat and listened all through with his face just beaming with satisfaction, and when the curtain fell at the close of Irving's grand presentation of the play, he stood up in his seat and cheered and yelled to his friends: "That's it! That's him! Didn't you see that man that came on the stage all the time and sort of put the whole play through, though you couldn't understand a word he said? Well, that's him! That's Saloonio!"

Telling His Faults

"Oh, do, Mr. Sapling," said the beautiful girl at the summer hotel, "do let me read the palm of your hand! I can tell you all your faults."

Mr. Sapling gave an inarticulate gurgle and a roseate flush swept over his countenance as he surrendered his palm to the grasp of the fair enchantress.

"Oh, you're just full of faults, just full of them, Mr. Sapling!" she cried.

Mr. Sapling looked it.

"To begin with," said the beautiful girl, slowly and reflectingly, "you are dreadfully cynical: you hardly believe in anything at all, and you've utterly no faith in us poor women."

The feeble smile that had hitherto kindled the features of Mr. Sapling into a ray of chastened imbecility, was distorted in an effort at cynicism.

"Then your next fault is that you are too determined; much too determined. When once you have set your will on any object, you crush every obstacle under your feet."

Mr. Sapling looked meekly down at his tennis shoes, but began to feel calmer, more lifted up. Perhaps he had been all these things without knowing it.

"Then you are cold and sarcastic."

Mr. Sapling attempted to look cold and sarcastic. He succeeded in a rude leer.

"And you're horribly world-weary, you care for nothing. You have drained philosophy to the dregs, and scoff at everything."

Mr. Sapling's inner feeling was that from now on he would simply scoff and scoff and scoff.

"Your only redeeming quality is that you are generous. You have tried to kill even this, but cannot. Yes," concluded the beautiful girl, "those are your faults, generous still, but cold, cynical and relentless. Good night, Mr. Sapling."

And resisting all entreaties the beautiful girl passed from the verandah of the hotel and vanished.

And when later in the evening the brother of the beautiful girl borrowed Mr. Sapling's tennis racket, and his bicycle for a fortnight, and the father of the beautiful girl got Sapling to endorse his note for a couple of hundreds, and her uncle Zephas borrowed his bedroom candle and used his razor to cut up a plug of tobacco, Mr. Sapling felt proud to be acquainted with the family.

Impervious to Women

"I look on myself," said Baffy Sims, "as a man impervious to women." He wasn't really a man; he was a fourth year undergraduate. But it's often hard to tell them apart.

He said this to me one afternoon on the campus just after lectures, but of course I'd heard Baffy Sims say it ever so many times before. Indeed, it was part of a set of fixed ideas; that he was impervious to women; that women were after him; but that they couldn't get him. He always felt and said that a fellow had to be pretty careful. He kept away from clergymen's houses, full of daughters, and never went to teas, lawn parties, nor any fool stuff of that sort. No sir! Not for him. In fact, that was why we called him "Baffy" Sims, because he used to say that he wished he could go up and live in Baffin Land where there were no women.

All men, as they get old, say things over and over. Sims started young. So we called him "Baffinland" Sims, and then just "Baffy." You know how names get stuck on a fellow at college and stay there. No, no, never mind telling me about the funny one you remember from your own college. Keep that for another treat.

At any rate this was the afternoon of the evening when Baffy was to read his paper to the Physico-Mathematical Society on the *Natural Inferiority of Women.*

"Be sure to come," he said. "I've got the paper nearly finished. It's a corker. I may give it to the *Atlantic.*"

"Oh, don't give it," I said. "Make them pay for it."

"Well, anyway," he said, "it's a corker."

Just then there came scurrying to us such a pretty girl, with a great armful of books tied up with a string. You and I would have noticed at once her beautiful violet eyes, but of course a fellow like Baffy wouldn't see them.

"Baffy!" she said, "I've just caught you in time! Look, I'm going out with Walter to play golf, so you take these books and sling them in at my house as you go by. Tell mother I'll be late . . . If mother's not there, go round to the back door and knock twice and Dinah'll come . . . That's good of you, Baffy."

She was off, leaving Baffy standing there with the armful of books.

"Who," I said with enthusiasm, "is that beautiful girl? Did you notice her eyes –"

"Eyes, hell," he said. "I'm impervious to that sort of thing. That's Pinkie Mordaunt, and I don't go past her house and she knows it. It's half a mile across the park. I told Mrs. Mordaunt last week to tell Pinkie I wouldn't take her books home any more."

"And what did she say?"

"I don't think she quite understood. She said to just give them to Dinah without coming to the front door at all . . . and look now today, with my paper to finish . . . Oh, well, come along . . ."

We had hardly got started when another college girl came fluttering to him. "Baffy," she said, "didn't you hear me call? I was hunting you all over the campus." She handed him a long envelope or rather she stuffed it under the string of Pinkie's books. "Here they are," she said. "I can't work the damn things."

"Quadratics, Dulcie?" said Baffy. Of course he was a real mathematician and could sense an equation even through an envelope.

"I don't know what the hell they are," Dulcie said. "They're what he gave us today."

A college girl always calls her professor simply "he." Some of them are not, but that's what they call them.

"I've got to hand them in at nine tomorrow. You're certainly a real sport, Baffy." "I'm not," Baffy began angrily, but she was gone.

Things never happen singly, or even doubly. So I knew that when I saw a third girl with a bulldog on a leash that there was still more coming for Baffy.

"Lucky meeting you, Baffy," she said.

"I can't take him, Anastasia," he said.

"Yes, you can," she protested. "I want to play tennis with Billy Hyde and I've just no time to take Churchill home . . ."

"Look here, Anastasia, the last time I took Churchill . . ."

"Don't be silly. Last time he hadn't been fed properly – no wonder he bit that boy – anyway Churchill's like that . . . Take him!" she said. And he did.

So that was that.

I'm not awfully keen on bulldogs. Oh, they're faithful! I

admit it – and quiet; a bulldog never bites. Oh, no – but I had to go another way anyway so I left Baffy with the dog.

But Baffy got even with them that night at the Physico-Mathematical Society when he read his paper on the *Natural Inferiority of Women*. They said it was a scorcher; and, mind you, they're accustomed in that society to scorch something every week – Monarchy, Christianity, God – things like that. I understand that Baffy showed that women lacked not only brains, but also leadership. In fact he didn't leave them a leg to – or, well, no, that's not exactly the metaphor. I won't say that.

Such was Baffy Sims path at college, impervious, as he said, to women. Not that there was anything mean-spirited about him. I don't imply that for a minute . . . And, of course, he couldn't help it if he knew a lot of girls and if they all called him Baffy. You see, his family had been in the city for ever so long and were well off and knew everybody. So of course the girls paid no attention to Baffy being impervious to women. To them he was just Baffy Sims.

Being well off, life was easy for Baffy in the material sense. He slid easily through Arts and through Law, a subject beyond the range of women, and slid easily as a barrister into a law business, since there was enough family and estate business to start it anyway . . .

"I've always felt impervious to women," he would say, "ever since I was a boy at college." He'd forgotten about being a man there . . .

But he was a pleasant fellow and life used him easily. Some people, clergymen's wives, said that it was a pity he hadn't married and that they must ask him up to tea . . . So you see there was something in his apprehension after all.

Anyway, his law practice opened out in pleasant and comfortable surroundings as I can testify.

"Come down and see my new offices some day," he said. "I've got everything running fine."

"It'll have to be early in the morning," I said.

"Early as you like," he answered, "or come down with me at nine-thirty."

So the next morning we arrived at the office – a pretty handsome place, I could see at the first glimpse through the open door – at 9:30 A.M. But Mrs. Murphy was still there. You know who Mrs. Murphy is – she's that big woman with the scrubbing pail and brush who is always in a law office before it opens — at her biggest because she's always on all fours and seen from the southwest . . .

"I can't let yez in yet, Mr. Sims," she said. "I've another half hour before I can let you have the office . . . Such a litter, such a dust. Now yous wait outside, half an hour, mebbe . . ."

"No, no, Mrs. Murphy," said Baffy, "never mind it now. It'll do fine as it is . . ."

"I might give the offices a touch-up after five," suggested Mrs. Murphy.

"Yes," said Baffy, "that's the idea," and I heard the rustle of a dollar bill passing to Mrs. Murphy, where all rustle ended . . .

"Yes, five o'clock."

"A fine woman," said Baffy as we went into his luxurious offices and sat down. "A fine woman — devoted to her work. Do you know that this is the third morning running that she's been working away over time like that . . . of course, a woman in that class accepts leadership. That woman looks to me . . ."

"She does," I said.

Baffy had hardly begun to show me the office fittings, the law books all in a row — the charm which even law has when young — when the new telephone sounded on the new desk . . .

"Yes, Miss Macarty," said Baffy . . .

"Yes . . . can't come to the office this morning, yes . . ."

"Why, certainly, Miss Macarty; yes . . ."

"Yes . . ."

"Your father's foot? Miss Macarty, why, yes, Miss Macarty . . ."

"Much wiser, yes — take him to Muskoka, yes . . ."

"No, Miss Macarty . . ."

"Back Monday, yes, Miss Macarty, yes . . ."

"Your golf kit? . . . Get it at your house, yes, and send it to Muskoka . . . I prepay it? Yes, yes. See you Monday — good."

"Miss Macarty," he explained, "my secretary. It's her father's gout again. He's a martyr to it. She won't be down this morning because of it. I'm sorry; I'd like you to have met her. A fine girl, and I will say, devoted to her work, never misses — except of course for a thing like this . . . She's her father's sole support outside of what he has of his own."

"And what about his gout?"

Feast of Stephen

"Wretched business, isn't it? Ever had it? Terribly painful . . . comes in sudden attacks . . ."

"And he's got it again?"

"No," said Baffy, "not yet. She wants to forestall it, but it's coming on; she feels it. Often she knows it before he does. Two weeks ago she had to rush him to Preston Springs for the week-end. Last week she rushed him to the Buffalo Races, just in time to ward off an attack. Today she's going to try to make Muskoka – the new hotel there – just in time. That's why she wants me to get her golf kit and send it by express . . . I must remember . . ."

Mrs. Murphy appeared at the door.

"Them ladies," she said, "is downstaris . . ."

"Tell them I'll come and bring them up," said Baffy hurriedly. "Now I'm sorry, –"

"Clients?" I said. "I'll get right out."

"No," he answered, "not exactly . . . It's the Women's Auxiliary Bazaar . . . they're bringing tickets . . . They want me to take a block of two hundred . . . women always imagine that men have more leadership in getting tickets – in fact they said so yesterday . . . Perhaps you'll buy one . . ."

"What's it for?" I asked.

"I don't know," he answered. "Some damn thing."

I saw quite a lot of Baffinland Sims that winter. He was prospering, as he deserved to do, good fellow, and life, except for his silly "impervious" fad, was all bright in front of him. He went out quite a lot into society. I'll never forget the speech he made at Pinkie Mordaunt's wedding, a speech on behalf of bachelors – I wish I could remember it; it was darned good . . . But mostly he went to bachelor gatherings, stag parties. In fact, that was when he founded the U.B.F., the United Bachelors Front, for resisting to the last man. The girls called it – or, well, you can't repeat what girls call that sort of thing.

So there was Baffinland Sims all headed straight for everlasting bachelordom. To think how easily such things end and break! Who could have imagined it all over by that next June? You could? Well, yes, but I mean who else but yourself?

Anyway, you know what the month of June is – all green and soft, all trees and garden and flowers – and every city suburb as fresh as a leafy forest . . . You know what June is; now take a June garden party, under the trees out on a big lawn . . . in one of those lovely big houses where the city ends and the country begins. Fill in tables scattered over the grass and sandwiches and jellies, and ices and drinks and bottles . . . and bevies of girls in all the colours of the flowers . . . and men in soft flannels – if you want a man to look a real man put him in soft flannel, or loose wool – people moving about in little knots and then untieing the knots to move somewhere else. By that means, you see, you get a drink here and then another drink there . . . and nobody counts them . . . Put in, of course – I was forgetting it – a band, seated around under a big tree and playing while the people move round and have drinks, and then the people stop moving and the band have drinks, and so on. You know what a garden party is on a lawn in June! Does a chicken sandwich ever taste so well? Does a cut of cold ham ever look more enticing? Pop! Bang! God Bless me! Champagne! Well! Here's luck!

And mind you it wasn't in *aid* of anything either . . . No, sir.

Well, Baffinland Sims was at the garden party, because he liked to go to that sort of thing. Just to laugh at it . . . It amused him.

So while he was at the height of his amusement at it, I was walking with him through the grounds, and he stopped all of a sudden and clutched my arm and said,

"Who is that marvellous looking girl?"

I didn't see any marvellous looking girl so I said, "Where?"

"There, in white, beside the end of that table!"

I looked and there wasn't any marvellous looking girl. I mean, there was only Molly Sheppardson. I'm not saying anything against Molly but you'll understand what I mean when I say that that's what it was, just Molly Sheppardson; only her. Molly's all right; a little large, you might say and, at a guess, going to be larger – you know the kind, the girls I mean. So I said,

"It's Molly Sheppardson." Of course, I didn't "only" to him. "I'll introduce you if you like."

"Do," he said, and then, "just a minute," and he began to fumble with his tie, and dust crumbs off himself that weren't there . . .

So I took Baffy over and I introduced him . . .

"How do you do?" Molly said; she speaks easily, I will say. "How do you do? Isn't everything beautifully green?"

I could see that Baffinland was impressed. Here was a girl

with a real reach of intellect! Her apprehension of greenness was wonderful.

I left them and wandered on to another table, where a girl I knew said, "How beautifully green everything is," and the man with her murmured "Spring . . ." He was a college man and had just come out first at graduation, so he knew. We had a drink together and then some more people came floating along and saying, "How beautifully green everything is, isn't it?"

But as I moved about I kept track of Baffy. I could see that he never left Molly Sheppardson. They were drifting round from table to table, and when I joined them for a minute Molly Sheppardson said to me, "How beautiful the flowers are!" And Baffinland Sims said to me, "Miss Sheppardson has just been remarking how green everything is . . ."

I saw them presently drifting away from the tables. Baffinland told me after that he had taken Miss Sheppardson on to look at the old well in the hollow at the bottom of the lawn; he said he didn't want her to miss seeing that. Yes, that would have been awful, wouldn't it, if Miss Sheppardson had not seen that well. But she saw it. I know she did because I watched them both standing there and peering down deep. I think I know what they saw.

Anyway, everybody saw it. It was just as plain as that . . . From the day after the garden party wherever Molly Sheppardson was, there was Baffinland Sims . . . In fact, it's so old a story that it's scarcely worth the telling.

Run smooth? Oh, smooth as spring and soft as summer and mellow as Autumn! Except for one slight interference that pulled it up short, or threatened to. Baffy Sims was going to propose to Molly Sheppardson; he knew it and I knew it because he said so. Then, I don't remember whether gradually or suddenly, he was brought up short by doubt whether he was worthy of her! There was the trouble. Think of it; if it turned out that he wasn't worthy of her – and he admitted that he wasn't fit to black her boots – but they were tan anyway . . . "Women," he explained to me while admitting that I wouldn't understand, "women are so much above men, in practically everything that really matters . . ."

However, it was all right. It turned out he *was* worthy. You see, he did propose to Molly – we won't mind details – and after she had said yes, old Mr. Sheppardson, Molly's father – he's a stock broker – looked into the question of what

Baffy was worth. He looked into it down town – and when he came up to the house he welcomed Baffy for a son-in-law with tears in his eyes . . . Old Mr. Sheppardson has done business with those tears in his eyes for forty years. If they were there, the thing was all right.

The wedding was certainly happy . . . The United Bachelors tried to raise a laugh at the wedding breakfast . . . Poor Simps! What did Baffy care!

The proof of it was that the marriage went on being happy . . . There was no story, no tragedy about it. After they were married I happened to be away from the city for some years but I heard all about it, – about their wonderful house in the suburbs, and the children, and Mrs. Sheppardson coming to live with them, and Molly – that's Mrs. Sims – being Head of the Women's Morning Musical (she made Baffy secretary) and President of the Women's Afternoon Dietetic, and the Women's Evening Endeavor, with Baffy as Honorary Vice President of each of them.

So when I returned to the city very naturally Baffy invited me out to his house to dine, and by good fortune it was again the month of June and the lovely place all at its best.

"You remember my wife," said Baffy proudly, as we shook hands. There was indeed plenty to be proud of – at least three sizes larger. "How beautifully green everything is," said Mrs. Sims.

Before dinner Baffy took me up to his "den" for a cigarette – the cutest little den you ever saw – his wife arranged it – away off up on the top of the house under the eaves – it used to be a pigeon house. That's where he smokes. Isn't that a good idea? It keeps the tobacco clear out of the house . . .

We went down again after the cigarette.

"The children," said Baffin, as the five little girls trouped in to shake hands – Delia, Belia, Phelia – no, I can't remember their names. Anyway, names like that. Perhaps there weren't five; it may have been four or six – nice little things, all so neat and pretty – and the oldest one said to me, "The flowers are lovely, aren't they?"

Then Baffy said, "My mother-in-law, Mrs. Sheppardson – and my wife's aunt, Miss Copperfax" – then he turned to his wife and asked, "Is great-grandmama coming down?"

"Not till after dinner," said his wife.

"I'm sorry," said Baffy and he explained. "My wife's grandmother, old Mrs. Sheppardson, lives with us . . . she's eighty-eight and just as bright as ever but she seldom comes down to dinner. All she takes in the evening is brandy and water and biscuits, and as my wife never likes any drink served in the dining room, we just send it up to her."

As he spoke, I saw a maid moving away with a decanter on a tray!

"Hey! Stop!" (I thought).

The Apology
of a Professor: An Essay
on Modern Learning

I know no more interesting subject of speculation, nor any more calculated to allow of a fair-minded difference of opinion, than the enquiry whether a professor has any right to exist. *Prima facie*, of course, the case is heavily against him. His angular overcoat, his missing buttons, and his faded hat, will not bear comparison with the double-breasted splendour of the stock-broker, or the *Directoire* fur gown of the cigar-maker. Nor does a native agility of body compensate for the missing allurement of dress. He cannot skate. He does not shoot. He must not swear. He is not brave. His mind, too, to the outsider at any rate, appears defective and seriously damaged by education. He cannot appreciate a twenty-five-cent novel, or a melodrama, or a moving-picture show, or any of that broad current of intellectual movement which soothes the brain of the business man in its moments of in-activity. His conversation, even to the tolerant, is impossible. Apparently he has neither ideas nor enthusiasms, nothing but an elaborate catalogue of dead men's opinions, which he cites with a petulant and peevish authority that will not brook contradiction, and that must be soothed by a tolerating acquiescence, or flattered by a plenary acknowledgement of ignorance.

Yet the very heaviness of this initial indictment against the professor might well suggest to an impartial critic that there must at least be mitigating circumstances in the case. Even if we are to admit that the indictment is well founded, the reason is all the greater for examining the basis on which it rests. At any rate some explanation of the facts involved may perhaps serve to palliate, if not to remove, demerits which are rather to be deplored than censured. It is one of the standing defects of our age that social classes, or let us say more narrowly, social categories, know so little of one an-other. For the purposes of ready reckoning, of that handy transaction of business which is the passion of the hour, we have adopted a way of labelling one another with the tag mark of a profession or an occupation that becomes an aid to business but a barrier to intercourse. This man is a professor, that man an "insurance man," a third – *terque quaterque beatus* – a "liquor man"; with these are "railroad men," "newspaper men," "dry goods men," and so forth. The things that we handle for our livelihood impose themselves upon our personality, till the very word "man" drops out, and a gentleman is referred to as a "heavy pulp and paper interest" while another man is a prominent "rubber plant"; two or three men round a dinner table become an "iron and steel circle," and thus it is that for the simple conception of a human being is substituted a complex of "interests," "rings," "circles," "sets," and other semi-geometrical figures arising out of avocations rather than affinities. Hence it comes that insurance men mingle with insurance men, liquor men mix, if one may use the term without afterthought, with liquor men: what looks like a lunch between three men at a club is really a cigar having lunch with a couple of plugs of tobacco.

Now the professor more than any ordinary person finds himself shut out from the general society of the business world. The rest of the "interests' have, after all, some things in common. The circles intersect at various points. Iron and steel has a certain fellowship with pulp and paper, and the whole lot of them may be converted into the common ground of preference shares and common stock. But the professor is to all of them an outsider. Hence his natural dissimilarity is unduly heightened in its appearance by the sort of avocational isolation in which he lives.

Let us look further into the status and the setting of the man. To begin with, history has been hard upon him. For some reason the strenuous men of activity and success in the drama of life have felt an instinctive scorn of the academic class, which they have been at no pains to conceal. Bismarck knew of no more bitter taunt to throw at the Free Trade economists of England than to say that they were all either clergymen or professors. Napoleon felt a life-long abhorrence of the class, broken only by one brief experiment that ended in failure. It is related that at the apogee of the Imperial rule, the idea flashed upon him that France must have learned men, that the professors must be encouraged. He decided to act at once. Sixty-five professors were invited that evening to the palace of the Tuileries. They came. They stood about in groups, melancholy and myopic beneath the light. Napoleon spoke to them in turn. To the first he spoke of fortifications. The professor in reply referred to the binomial theorem. "Put him out," said Napoleon. To the second he spoke of commerce. The professor in answer cited the opinions of Diodorus Siculus. "Put him out," said Napoleon. At the end of half an hour Napoleon had had enough of the professors. "Cursed idealogues," he cried; "put them all out." Nor were they ever again admitted.

Nor is it only in this way that the course of history has been unkind to the professor. It is a notable fact in the past, that all persons of eminence who might have shed a lustre upon the academic class are absolved from the title of professor, and the world at large is ignorant that they ever wore it. We never hear of the author of "The Wealth of Nations" as Professor Smith, nor do we know the poet of "Evangeline" as Professor Longfellow. The military world would smile to see the heroes of the Southern Confederacy styled Professor Lee and Professor Jackson. We do not know of Professor Harrison as the occupant of a President's chair. Those whose talk is of dreadnoughts and of strategy never speak of Professor Mahan, and France has long since forgotten the proper title of Professor Guizot and Professor Taine. Thus it is that the ingratitude of an undiscerning public robs the professional class of the honour of its noblest names. Nor does the evil stop there. For, in these latter days at least, the same public which eliminates the upward range of the term, applies it downwards and sideways with indiscriminating generality. It is a "professor" who plays upon the banjo. A "professor" teaches swimming. Hair-cutting, as an art, is imparted in New York by "professors"; while any gentleman whose thaumaturgic intercommunication with the world of spirits has reached the point of interest which warrants advertising space in the daily press, explains himself as a "professor" to his prospective clients. So it comes that the true professor finds all his poor little attributes of distinction – his mock dignity, his gown, his string of supplementary letters – all taken over by a mercenary age to be exploited, as the stock-in-trade of an up-to-date advertiser. The vendor of patent medicine depicts himself in the advertising columns in a gown, with an uplifted hand to show the Grecian draping of the fold. After his name are placed enough letters and full stops to make up a simultaneous equation in algebra.

The word "professor" has thus become a generic term, indicating the assumption of any form of dexterity, from hair-cutting to running the steam shovel in a crematorium. It is even customary – I am informed – to designate in certain haunts of meretricious gaiety the gentleman whose efforts at the piano are rewarded by a *per capita* contribution of ten cents from every guest – the "professor."

One may begin to see, perhaps, the peculiar disadvantage under which the professor labours in finding his avocation confused with the various branches of activity for which he can feel nothing but a despairing admiration. But there are various ways also in which the very circumstances of his profession cramp and bind him. In the first place there is no doubt that his mind is very seriously damaged by his perpetual contact with the students. I would not for a moment imply that a university would be better off without the students; although the point is one which might well elicit earnest discussion. But their effect upon the professor is undoubtedly bad. He is surrounded by an atmosphere of sycophantic respect. His students, on his morning arrival, remove his overshoes and hang up his overcoat. They sit all day writing down his lightest words with stylographic pens of the very latest model. They laugh at the meanest of his jests. They treat him with a finely simulated respect that has come down as a faint tradition of the old days of Padua and Bologna, when a professor was in reality the venerated master, a man who wanted to teach, and the students disciples who wanted to learn.

All that is changed now. The supreme import of the professor to the students now lies in the fact that he controls the examinations. He holds the golden key which will unlock the door of the temple of learning – unlock it, that is, not to let the student in, but to let him get out – into something decent. This fact gives to the professor a fictitious importance, easily confounded with his personality, similar to that of the gatekeeper at a dog show, or the ticket-wicket man at a hockey match.

In this is seen part of the consequences of the vast, organised thing called modern education. Everything has the merits of its defects. It is a grand thing and a possible thing, that practically all people should possess the intellectual-mechanical arts of reading, writing, and computation: good too that they should possess pigeon-holed and classified data of the geography and history of the world; admirable too that they should possess such knowledge of the principles of natural science as will enable them to put a washer on a kitchen tap, or inflate a motor tyre with a soda-syphon bottle. All this is splendid. This we have got. And this places us collectively miles above the rude illiterate men-of-arms, burghers, and villeins of the Middle Ages who thought the moon took its light from God, whereas we know that its light is simply a function of π divided by the square of its distance.

Let me not get confused in my thesis. I am saying that the universal distribution of mechanical education is a fine thing, and that we have also proved it possible. But above this is the utterly different thing – we have no good word for it, call it learning, wisdom, enlightenment, anything you will – which means not a mechanical acquirement from without but something done from within: a power and willingness to think: an interest, for its own sake, in that general enquiry into the form and meaning of life which constitutes the ground plan of education. Now this, desirable though it is, cannot be produced by the mechanical compulsion of organised education. It belongs, and always has, to the few and never to the many. The ability to think is rare. Any man can think and think hard when he has to: the savage devotes a nicety of thought to the equipoise of his club, or the business man to the adjustment of a market price. But the ability or desire to think without compulsion about things that neither warm the hands nor fill the stomach is very rare. Reflection on the riddle of life, the cruelty of death, the innate savagery and the sublimity of the creature man, the history and progress of man in his little earth-dish of trees and flowers – all these things taken either "straight" in the masculine form of philosophy and the social sciences, or taken by diffusion through the feminised form literature, constitute the operation of the educated mind. Of all these things most people in their degree think a little and then stop. They realise presently that these things are very difficult, and that they don't matter, and that there is no money in them. Old men never think of them at all. They are glad enough to stay in the warm daylight a little longer. For a working solution of these problems different things are done. Some people use a clergyman. Others declare that the Hindoos know all about it. Others, especially of late, pay a reasonable sum for the services of a professional thaumaturgist who supplies a solution of the soul problem by mental treatment at long range, radiating from State Street, Chicago. Others, finally, of a native vanity that will not admit itself vanquished, buckle about themselves a few little formulas of "evolution" and "force," co-relate the conception of God to the differentiation of a frog's foot, and strut through life emplumed with the rump-feathers of their own conceit.

I trust my readers will not think that I have forgotten my

professor. I have not. All of this digression is but an instance of *reculer pour mieux sauter*. It is necessary to bring out all this background of the subject to show the setting in which the professor is placed. Possibly we shall begin to see that behind this quaint being in his angular overcoat are certain greater facts in respect to the general relation of education to the world of which the professor is only a product, and which help to explain, if they do not remove, the dislocated misfit of his status among his fellow men. We were saying then that the truly higher education – thought about life, mankind, literature, art – cannot be handed out at will. To attempt to measure it off by the yard, to mark it out into stages and courses, to sell it at the commutation rate represented by a college sessional fee – all this produces a contradiction in terms. For the thing itself is substituted an imitation of it. For real wisdom – obtainable only by the few – is substituted a nickel-plated make-believe obtainable by any person of ordinary intellect who has the money, and who has also, in the good old Latin sense, the needful assiduity. I am not saying that the system is bad. It is the best we can get; and incidentally, and at back-rounds, it turns out a bye-product in the shape of a capable and well-trained man who has forgotten all about the immortality of the soul, in which he never had any interest any way, but who conducts a law business with admirable efficiency.

The result, then, of this odd-looking system is, that what ought to be a thing existing for itself is turned into qualification for something else. The reality of a student's studies is knocked out by the grim earnestness of having to pass an examination. How can a man really think of literature, or of the problem of the soul, who knows that he must learn the contents of a set of books in order to pass an examination which will give him the means of his own support and, perhaps, one-half the support of his mother, or fifteen per cent of that of a maiden aunt. The pressure of circumstances is too much. The meaning of study is lost. The qualification is everything.

Not that the student finds his burden heavy or the situation galling. He takes the situation as he finds it, is hugely benefited by it at back-rounds, and, being young, adapts himself to it: accepts with indifference whatever programme may be needful for the qualification that he wants: studies Hebrew or Choctaw with equal readiness; and as his education progresses, will write you a morning essay on transcendental utilitarianism, and be back again to lunch. At the end of his course he has learned much. He has learned to sit – that first requisite for high professional work – and he can sit for hours. He can write for hours with a stylographic pen: more than that, for I wish to state the case fairly, he can make a digest, or a summary, or a reproduction of anything in the world. Incidentally the *speculation* is all knocked sideways out of him. But the lack of it is never felt.

Observe that it was not so in Padua. The student came thither from afar off, on foot or on a mule; so I picture him at least in my ignorance of Italian history, seated droopingly upon a mule, with earnest brown eyes hungered with the desire to know, and in his hand a vellum-bound copy of Thomas Aquinas written in long-hand, priceless, as *he* thinks, for the wisdom it contains. Now the Padua student wanted to know: not for a qualification, not because he wanted to be a pharmaceutical expert with a municipal licence, but because he thought the things in Thomas Aquinas and such to be things of tremendous import. They were not; but he thought so. This student thought that he could really find out things: that if he listened daily to the words of the master who taught him, and read hard, and thought hard, he would presently discover real truths – the only things in life that he cared for – such as whether the soul is a fluid or a solid, whether his mule existed or was only a vapour, and much other of this sort. These things he fully expected to learn. For their sake he brought to bear on the person of his teacher that reverential admiration which survives faintly to-day, like a biological "vestige," in the attitude of the college student who holds the overcoat of his professor. The Padua student, too, got what he came for. After a time he knew all about the soul, all about his mule – knew, too, something of the more occult, the almost devilish sciences, perilous to tackle, such as why the sun is suspended from falling into the ocean, or the very demonology of symbolism – the AL-GEB of the Arabians – by which $X + Y$ taken to the double or square can be shown after many days' computation to be equal to $X^2 + 2XY + Y^2$.

A man with such knowledge simply *had* to teach it. What to him if he should wear a brown gown of frieze and feed on pulse! This, as beside the bursting force of the expanding steam of his knowledge, counted for nothing. So he went forth, and he in turn became a professor, a man of profound acquirement, whose control over malign comets elicited a shuddering admiration.

These last reflections seem to suggest that it is not merely that something has gone wrong with the attitude of the student and the professor towards knowledge, but that something has gone wrong with knowledge itself. We have got the thing into such a shape that we do not know one-tenth as much as we used to. Our modern scholarship has poked and pried in so many directions, has set itself to be so ultra-rational, so hyper-sceptical, that now it knows nothing at all. All the old certainty has vanished. The good old solid dogmatic dead-sureness that buckled itself in the oak and brass of its own stupidity is clean gone. It died at about the era of the country squire, the fox-hunting parson, the three-bottle Prime Minister, and the voluminous Doctor of Divinity in broadcloth imperturbable even in sobriety and positively omniscient when drunk. We have argued them off the stage of a world all too ungrateful. In place of their sturdy outlines appear that sickly anæmic Modern Scholarship, the double-jointed jack-in-the-box, Modern Religion, the feminine angularity of Modern Morality, bearing a jug of filtered water, and behind them, as the very lord of wisdom, the grinning mechanic, Practical Science, using the broadcloth suit of the defunct doctor as his engine-room overalls. Or if we prefer to place the same facts without the aid of personification, our learning has so watered itself down that the starch and consistency is all out of it. There is no absolute sureness anywhere. Everything is henceforth to be a development, an evolution; morals and ethics are turned from fixed facts to shifting standards that change from age to age like the fashion of our clothes; art and literature are only a product, not good or bad, but a part of its age and environment. So it comes that our formal studies are no longer a burning quest for absolute truth. We have long since discovered that we cannot know anything. Our studies consist only in the long-drawn proof of the futility for the search after knowledge effected by exposing the errors of the past. Philosophy is the science which proves that we can know nothing of the soul. Medicine is the science which tells that we know nothing of the body. Political Economy is that which teaches that we know nothing of the laws of wealth; and Theology the critical history of those errors from which we deduce our ignorance of God.

When I sit and warm my hands, as best I may, at the little heap of embers that is now Political Economy, I cannot but contrast its dying glow with the generous blaze of the vainglorious and triumphant science that once it was.

Such is the distinctive character of modern learning, imprint with a resigned agnosticism towards the search after truth, able to refute everything and to believe nothing, and leaving its once earnest devotees stranded upon the arid sands of their own ignorance. In the face of this fact can it be wondered that a university converts itself into a sort of mill, grinding out its graduates, legally qualified, with conscientious regularity? The students take the mill as they find it, perform their task and receive their reward. They listen to their professor. They write down with stylographic pens in loose-leaf note-books his most inane and his most profound speculations with an undiscriminating impartiality. The reality of the subject leaves but little trace upon their minds.

All of what has been said above has been directed mainly towards the hardship of the professor's lot upon its scholastic side. Let me turn to another aspect of his life, the moral. By a strange confusion of thought a professor is presumed to be a good man. His standing association with the young and the history of his profession, which was once amalgamated with that of the priesthood, give him a connexion at one remove with morality. He therefore finds himself in that category of men – including himself and the curate as its chief representatives – to whom the world at large insists on ascribing a rectitude of character and a simplicity of speech that unfits them for ordinary society. It is gratuitously presumed that such men prefer tea to whisky and soda, blind man's buff to draw poker, and a freshmen's picnic to a prize fight.

For the curate of course I hold no brief. Let him sink. In any case he has to console him the favour of the sex, a concomitant perhaps of his very harmlessness, but productive at the same time of creature comforts. Soft slippers deck his little feet, flowers lie upon his study table, and round his lungs the warmth of an embroidered chest-protector proclaims the favour of the fair. Of this the ill-starred professor shares nothing. It is a sad fact that he is at once harmless and despised. He may lecture for twenty years and never find so much as a mullein stalk upon his desk. For him no canvas slippers, knitted by fair fingers, nor the flowered gown, nor clock-worked hosiery of the ecclesiastic. The sex will have none of him. I do not mean, of course, that there are no women that form exceptions to this rule. We have all seen immolated upon the academic hearth, and married to professors, women whose beauty and accomplishments would have adorned the home of a wholesale liquor merchant. But the broad rule still obtains. Women who embody, so St. Augustine has told us, the very principle of evil, can only really feel attracted towards bad men. The professor is too good for them.

Whether a professor is of necessity a good man, is a subject upon which I must not presume to dogmatise. The women may be right in voting him a "muff." But if he is such in any degree, the conventional restrictions of his profession tend to heighten it. The bursts of profanity that are hailed as a mark of business energy on the part of a railway magnate or a cabinet minister are interdicted to a professor. It is a canon of his profession that he must never become violent, nor lift his hand in anger. I believe that it was not always so. The story runs, authentic enough, that three generations ago a Harvard professor in a fit of anger with a colleague (engendered, if I recall the case, by the discussion of a nice point in thermo-dynamics) threw him into a chemical furnace and burned him. But the buoyancy of those days is past. In spite of the existence of our up-to-date apparatus, I do not believe that any of our present professoriate has yielded to such an impulse.

One other point remains worthy of remark in the summation of the heavy disadvantages under which the professor lives and labours. He does not know how to make money. This is a grave fault, and one that in the circumstances of the day can scarcely be overlooked. It comes down to him as a legacy of the Padua days when the professor neither needed money nor thought of it. Now when he would like money he is hampered by an "evoluted" inability to get hold of it. He dares not commercialise his profession, or does not know how to do so. Had he the business instinct of the leaders of labour and the master manufacturers, he would long since have set to work at the problem. He would have urged his government to put so heavy a tax on the import of foreign professors as to keep the home market for himself. He would have organised himself into amalgamated Brotherhoods of Instructors of Latin, United Greek Workers of America, and so forth, organised strikes, picketed the houses of the college trustees, and made himself a respected place as a member of industrial society. This his inherited inaptitude forbids him to do.

Nor can the professor make money out of what he knows. Somehow a plague is on the man. A teacher of English cannot write a half-dime novel, nor a professor of dynamics invent a safety razor. The truth is that a modern professor for commercial purposes doesn't know anything. He only knows parts of things.

It occurred to me some years ago when the Cobalt silver mines were first discovered that a professor of scientific attainments ought to be able, by transferring his talent to that region, to amass an enormous fortune. I questioned one of the most gifted of my colleagues. "Could you not," I asked, "as a specialist in metals discover silver mines at sight?" "Oh, no," he said, shuddering at the very idea, "you see I'm only a metallurgist; at Cobalt the silver is all in the rocks and I know nothing of rocks whatever." "Who then," I asked "knows about rocks?" "For that," he answered, "you need a geologist like Adamson; but then you see, he knows the rocks, but doesn't know the silver." "But could you not both go," I said, "and Adamson hold the rock while you extracted the silver?" "Oh, no," the professor answered, "you see we are neither of us mining engineers; and even then we ought to have a good hydraulic man and an electric man." "I suppose," I said, "that if I took about seventeen of you up there you might find something. No? Well, would it not be possible to get somebody who would know something of *all* these things?" "Yes," he said, "any of the fourth year students would, but personally all that I do is to reduce the silver when I get it." "That I can do myself," I answered musingly, and left him.

Such then is the professor; a man whose avocation in life is hampered by the history of its past: imparting in the form of statutory exercises knowledge that in its origin meant a spontaneous effort of the intelligence, whose very learning itself has become a profession rather than a pursuit, whose mock dignity and fictitious morality remove him from the society of his own sex and deny to him the favour of the other. Surely, in this case, to understand is to sympathise. Is it not possible, too, that when all is said and done the professor is performing a useful service in the world, unconsciously of course, in acting as a leaven in the lump of commercialism that sits so heavily on the world to-day? I do not wish to expand upon this theme. I had set out to make the apology of the professor speak for itself from the very circumstances of his work. But in these days, when money is everything, when pecuniary success is the only goal to be achieved, when the voice of the plutocrat is as the voice of God, the aspect of the professor, side-tracked in the real race of life, riding his mule of Padua in competition with an automobile, may at least help to soothe the others who have failed in the struggle.

Dare one, as the wildest of fancies, suggest how different things might be if learning counted, or if we could set it on its feet again, if students wanted to learn, and if professors had anything to teach, if a university lived for itself and not as a place of qualification for the junior employees of the rich; if there were only in this perplexing age some way of living humbly and retaining the respect of one's fellows; if a man with a few hundred dollars a year could cast out the money question and the house question, and the whole business of competitive appearances and live for the things of the mind! But then, after all, if the mind as a speculative instrument has gone bankrupt, if learning, instead of meaning a mind full of thought, means only a bellyful of fact, one is brought to a full stop, standing among the littered débris of an ideal that has passed away.

In any case the question, if it is one, is going to settle itself. The professor is passing away. The cost of living has laid its hold upon him, and grips him in its coils; within another generation he will be starved out, frozen out, "evoluted" out by that glorious process of natural selection and adaptation, the rigour of which is the only God left in our desolated Pantheon. The male schoolteacher is gone, the male clerk is going, and already on the horizon of the academic market rises the Woman with the Spectacles, the rude survivalist who, in the coming generation, will dispense the elements of learning cut to order, without an afterthought of what it once has meant.

My Memories
and Miseries
as a Schoolmaster

For ten years I was a schoolmaster. Just thirty years ago I was appointed to the staff of a great Canadian school. It took me ten years to get off it. Being appointed to the position of a teacher is just as if Fate passed a hook through one's braces and hung one up against the wall. It is hard to get down again.

From those ten years I carried away nothing in money and little in experience; indeed, no other asset whatever, unless it be, here and there, a pleasant memory or two and the gratitude of my former pupils. There was nothing really in my case for them to be grateful about. They got nothing from me in the way of intellectual food, but a lean and perfunctory banquet; and anything that I gave them in the way of sound moral benefit I gave gladly and never missed.

But school boys have a way of being grateful. It is the decent thing about them. A school boy, while he is at school, regards his masters as a mixed assortment of tyrants and freaks. He plans vaguely that at some future time in life he will "get even" with them. I remember well, for instance, at the school where I used to teach, a little Chilian boy who kept a stiletto in his trunk with which he intended to kill the second mathematical master.

But somehow a schoolboy is no sooner done with his school and out in the business of life, than a soft haze of retrospect suffuses a new color over all that he has left behind. There is a mellow sound in the tones of the school bell that he never heard in his six years of attendance. There is a warmth in the color of the old red bricks that he never saw before; and such a charm and such a sadness in the brook or in the elm trees beside the school playground that he will stand beside them with a bowed and reverent head as in the silence of a cathedral. I have seen an "Old Boy" gaze into the open door of an empty class room and ask, "And those are the same old benches?" with a depth of meaning in his voice. He has been out of school perhaps five years and the benches already seem to him infinitely old. This, by the way, is the moment and this the mood in which the "Old Boy" may be touched for a subscription to the funds of the school. This *is* the way in fact, in which the sagacious head master does it. The foolish head master, who has not yet learned his business, takes the "Old Boy" round and shows him all the *new* things, the fine new swimming pool built since his day and the new gymnasium with up-to-date patent apparatus. But this is all wrong. There is nothing in it for the "Old Boy" but boredom. The wise head master takes him by the sleeve and says "Come"; he leads him out to a deserted corner of the playground and shows him an old tree behind an ash house and the "Old Boy" no sooner sees it than he says:

"Why, Great Caesar! that's the same old tree that Jack McEwen and I used to climb up to hook out of bounds on Saturday night! Old Jimmy caught us at it one night and licked us both. And look here, here's my name cut on the boarding at the back of the ash house. See? They used to fine us five cents a letter if they found it. Well, Well!"

The "Old Boy" is deep in his reminiscences examining the board fence, the tree and the ash house.

The wise head master does not interrupt him. He does not say that he knew all along that the "Old Boy's" name was cut there and that that's why he brought him to the spot. Least of all does he tell him that the boys still "hook out of bounds" by this means and that he licked two of them for it last Saturday night. No, no, retrospect is too sacred for that. Let the "Old Boy" have his fill of it and when he is quite down and out with the burden of it, then as they walk back to the school building, the head master may pick a donation from him that falls like a ripe thimbleberry.

And most of all, by the queer contrariety of things, does this kindly retrospect envelop the person of the teachers. They are transported in the alchemy of time into a group of profound scholars, noble benefactors through whose teaching, had it been listened to, one might have been lifted into higher things. Boys who never listened to a Latin lesson in their lives look back to the memory of their Latin teacher as the one great man that they have known. In the days when he taught them they had no other idea than to put mud in his ink or to place a bent pin upon his chair. Yet they say now that he was the greatest scholar in the world and that if they'd only listened to him they would have got more out of his lessons than from any man that ever taught. He wasn't and they wouldn't — but it is some small consolation to those who have been schoolmasters to know that after it is too late this reward at least is coming to them.

Hence it comes about that even so indifferent a vessel as I should reap my share of schoolboy gratitude. Again and again it happens to me that some unknown man, well on in middle life, accosts me with a beaming face and says: "You don't remember me. You licked me at Upper Canada College," and we shake hands with a warmth and heartiness as if I had been his earliest benefactor. Very often if I am at an evening reception or anything of the sort, my hostess says, "Oh, there is a man here so anxious to meet you," and I know at once why. Forward he comes, eagerly pushing his way among the people to seize my hand. "Do you remember me?" he says. "You licked me at Upper Canada College." Sometimes I anticipate the greeting. As soon as the stranger grasps my hand and says, "Do you remember me?" I break in and say, "Why, let me see, surely I licked you at Upper Canada College." In such a case the man's delight is beyond all bounds. Can I lunch with him at his Club? Can I dine at his home? He wants his wife to see me. He has so often told her about having been licked by me that she too will be delighted.

I do not like to think that I was in any way brutal or harsh, beyond the practice of my time, in beating the boys I taught. Looking back on it, the whole practice of licking and being licked, seems to me mediaeval and out of date. Yet I do know that there are, apparently, boys that I have licked in all quarters of the globe. I get messages from them. A man says to me, "By the way, when I was out in Sumatra there was a man there that said he knew you. He said you licked him at Upper Canada College. He said he often thought of you." I have licked, I believe, two Generals of the Canadian Army, three Cabinet Ministers, and more Colonels and Mayors than I care to count. Indeed all the boys that I have licked seem to be doing well.

I am stating here what is only simple fact, not exaggerated a bit. Any schoolmaster and every "Old Boy" will recognize it at once; and indeed I can vouch for the truth of this feeling on the part of the "Old Boys" all the better in that I have felt it myself. I always read Ralph Connor's books with great interest for their own sake, but still more because, thirty-two years ago, the author "licked me at Upper Canada College." I have never seen him since, but I often say to people from Winnipeg, "If you ever meet Ralph Connor – he's Major Charles Gordon, you know – tell him that I was asking about him and would like to meet him. He licked me at Upper Canada College."

But enough of "licking." It is, I repeat, to me nowadays a

painful and a disagreeable subject. I can hardly understand how we could have done it. I am glad to believe that at the present time it has passed or is passing out of use. I understand that it is being largely replaced by "moral suasion." This, I am sure, is a great deal better. But when I was a teacher moral suasion was just beginning at Upper Canada College. In fact I saw it tried only once. The man who tried it was a tall, gloomy-looking person, a university graduate in psychology. He is now a well-known Toronto lawyer, so I must not name him. He came to the school only as a temporary substitute for an absent teacher. He was offered a cane by the College janitor whose business it was to hand them round. But he refused it. He said that a moral appeal was better: he said that psychologically it set up an inhibition stronger than the physical. The first day that he taught – it was away up in a little room at the top of the old college building on King Street – the boys merely threw paper wads at him and put bent pins on his seat. The next day they put hot bees-wax on his clothes and the day after that they brought screw drivers and unscrewed the little round seats of the class room and rolled them down the stairs. After that day the philosopher did not come back, but he has since written, I believe, a book called "Psychic Factors in Education"; which is very highly thought of.

But the opinion of the "Old Boy" about his teachers is only a part of his illusionment. The same peculiar haze of retrospect hangs about the size and shape and kind of boys who went to school when he was young as compared with the boys of to-day.

"How small they are!" is always the exclamation of the "Old Boy" when he looks over the rows and rows of boys sitting in the assembly hall. "Why, when I went to school the boys were ever so much bigger."

After which he goes on to relate that when he first entered the school as a youngster (the period apparently of maximum size and growth), the boys in the sixth form had whiskers! These whiskers of the sixth form are a persistent and perennial school tradition that never dies. I have traced them, on personal record from eye-witnesses, all the way from 1829, when the college was founded, until to-day. I remember well, during my time as a schoolmaster, receiving one day a parent, an "Old Boy" who came accompanied by a bright little son of twelve whom he was to enter at the school. The boy was sent to play about with some new acquaintances while I talked with his father.

"The old school," he said in the course of our talk, "is greatly changed, very much altered. For one thing the boys are very much younger than they were in my time. Why, when I entered the school – though you will hardly believe it – the boys in the sixth form had whiskers!"

I had hardly finished expressing my astonishment and appreciation when the little son came back and went up to his father's side and started whispering to him. "Say, dad," he said, "there are some awfully big boys in this school. I saw out there in the hall some boys in the sixth form with whiskers."

From which I deduced that what is whiskers to the eye of youth fades into fluff before the disillusioned eye of age. Nor is there need to widen the application or to draw the moral.

The parents of the boys at school naturally fill a broad page in the schoolmaster's life and are responsible for many of his sorrows. There are all kinds and classes of them. Most acceptable to the schoolmaster is the old-fashioned type of British father who enters his boy at the school and says:

"Now I want this boy well thrashed if he doesn't behave himself. If you have any trouble with him let me know and I'll come and thrash him myself. He's to have a shilling a week pocket money and if he spends more than that let me know and I'll stop his money altogether." Brutal though this speech sounds, the real effect of it is to create a strong prejudice in the little boy's favor and when his father curtly says, "Good-bye, Jack," and he answers, "Good-bye father," in a trembling voice, the schoolmaster would be a hound indeed who could be unkind to him.

But very different is the case of the up-to-date parent. "Now I've just given Jimmy fifty dollars," he says to the schoolmaster with the same tone as he would to an inferior clerk in his office, "and I've explained to him that when he wants more he's to tell you to go to the bank and draw for him what he needs." After which he goes on to explain that Jimmy is a boy of very peculiar disposition, requiring the greatest nicety of treatment; that they find if he gets in tempers the best way is to humor him and presently he'll come round. Jimmy, it appears can be led, if led gently, but never driven. During all of which time the schoolmaster, insulted by being treated as an underling, (for the iron bites deep into the soul of every one of them), has already fixed his eye on the undisciplined young pup called Jimmy with a view to trying out the problem of seeing whether he can't be driven after all.

But the greatest nuisance of all to the schoolmaster is the parent who does his boy's home exercises and works his boy's sums. I suppose they mean well by it. But it is a disastrous thing to do for any child. Whenever I found myself correcting exercises that had obviously been done for the boys in their homes I used to say to them quite grandly:

"Paul, tell your father that he *must* use the ablative after pro."

"Yes, sir," says the boy.

"And Edward, you tell your grandmother that her use of the dative case simply won't do. She's getting along nicely and I'm well satisfied with the way she's doing, but I cannot have her using the dative right and left on every occasion. Tell her it won't do."

"Yes, sir," says little Edward.

I remember one case in particular of a parent who did not do the boy's exercise but, after letting the boy do it himself, wrote across the face of it a withering comment addressed to me and reading: "From this exercise you can see that my boy, after six months of your teaching, is completely ignorant. How do you account for it?"

I sent the exercise back to him with the added note: "I think it must be hereditary."

In the whole round of the school year, there was, as I remember it, but one bright spot – the arrival of the summer holidays. Somehow as the day draws near for the school to break up for holidays, a certain touch of something human pervades the place. The masters lounge round in cricket flannels smoking cigarettes almost in the corridors of the school itself. The boys shout at their play in the long June evenings. At the hour when, on the murky winter nights, the bell rang for night study, the sun is still shining upon the playground and the cricket match between House and House is being played out between daylight and dark. The masters – good fellows that they are – have cancelled evening study to watch the game. The headmaster is there himself. He is smoking a briar-wood pipe and wearing his mortar-board sideways. There is wonderful greenness in the new grass of the playground and a wonderful fragrance in the evening air. It is the last day of school but one. Life is sweet indeed in the anticipation of this summer evening.

If every day in the life of a school could be the last day but one, there would be little fault to find with it.

Education Eating Up Life

Education longer and longer – Life ten years too late, and Death on time – Where we got our Curriculum – Mediaeval Schools with Modern Extension – A Scholar and a Gentleman, plus a Scientist and a Business Man – The Straws on the Camel's Back

In this discussion of education, I am addressing myself to plain people. By this I mean people who shudder at mathematics, go no further in Latin than *E Pluribus Unum* and take electricity as they find it. As opposed to these are the academic class who live in colleges, or in the shadow of them, and claim education as their province. But the plain people are of necessity interested in education because their sons and daughters go to college, or, more important, can't go to college.

Now the plain people have noticed that education is getting longer and longer. Fifty years ago people learned to read out of a spelling-book at six years old, went to high school at twelve, and taught school (for money) on a third-class certificate at sixteen. After that, two years in a saw-mill and two at a medical school made them doctors, or one year in a saw-mill and one in divinity fitted them for the church. For law they needed no college at all, just three summers on a farm and three winters in an office.

All our great men in North America got this education. Pragmatically, it worked. They began their real life still young. With the money they didn't spend they bought a wife. By the age of thirty they had got somewhere, or nowhere. It is true that for five years of married life, they carried, instead of a higher degree, bills for groceries, coal, doctors, and babies' medicine. Then they broke out of the woods, into the sunlight, established men – at an age when their successors are still demonstrating, interning, or writing an advanced thesis on social impetus.

Now it is all changed. Children in school at six years old

cut up paper dolls and make patterns. They are still in high school till eighteen, learning civics and social statistics – studies for old men. They enter college at about nineteen or twenty, take prerequisites and post-requisites in various faculties for nearly ten years, then become demonstrators, invigilators, researchers, or cling to a graduate scholarship like a man on a raft.

At thirty they are just beginning, ten years too late. They can't marry till it's ten years too late; they have children ten years too late, and die ten years too early. They know nothing of the early life of the man who worked in saw-mills, practiced medicine at twenty and married six months later, with no other property than a stethoscope and a horse and buggy; or of the young lawyer who married in debt, and lived happy in it ever after.

"Safety first" has put its stamp on life. Population begins to die at the top. And, all the time, education grows longer and longer. This does not deny that the average human life is now longer. It means that paternity is shorter. People do not see enough of their grandchildren – the sweetest prospect in the world. Life has all too little evening. It has all run in arrears and never catches up.

All this, you will say, is exaggerated, is overcolored, is not truth. Very likely. But a half truth in argument, like a half brick, carries better. High colors show up where neutral tints blend to nothing. Yet the main truth gets over. Education is eating up life.

In the above paragraphs I have formulated the plain man's accusations against the continued lengthening of education; or, rather, I must not say his accusation. The poor fellow hasn't the spirit to accuse. It is not an accusation that he formulates or a grievance that he voices. It is just a burden that he carries.

He carries it because of the prestige of education. Round the idea of education, as effort and opportunity, there have clustered centuries of tradition and association. These are stamped in such words and phrases as "the little red school-house," "the midnight oil," "the eager student," "the kindly dominie," "the absent-minded professor." With this has grown up the notion – no doubt partly true – that the harder the path of learning the higher the achievement. "There is no royal road to learning" still cheers those who are unaware that the public road itself has become overgrown with a jungle of underbrush.

In other words, people don't complain. On the contrary,

they are often proud of the burden that they carry. Parents have no regrets for the fifteen years of sacrifice that they made to give their children the education they should have had in half the time.

It is a tradition with us that education opens opportunity. To send a boy to college is an ambition that wakes to life beside a cradle. "How is your son doing at school, Mr. McGregor?" I once asked of a Scotsman of the traditional type. "Fine!" he answered. "If he keeps on as he is, we'll have to put the college to him."

Even in the clutter and failure of youth's career among the blocked avenues of our misfit world the college comes into its own as a sort of refuge. "My son," said another parent, "doesn't seem to have any particular ability, so we think we'll have to send him to college. He seems no good for anything else." The one anxiety of such parents is, "Can he get in?" Beyond that no need to look. It's like being dipped in the Jordan.

But even if the plain man were to raise his complaint against the lengthening road and the increasing burden, he would be laughed out of court by the academic class. He would be told that our education is all too short. The teachers in the high schools would say that the children come to them hopelessly unprepared and ought to stay a year longer in public school.

Every professor will tell them that the first-year students at college are simply hopeless and ought to have stayed at least a year, or call it two, at high school. The students in the second year ought never to have left the first; the third-year men haven't the proper grounding for their work; and the fourth-year are so rotten that they have to be given degrees to get rid of them. As for the graduate school, the students in it should never have been admitted; they are not yet fit for advanced work. Their minds are immature. And even when they do get out of the graduate school, by sheer lapse of time, it seems ridiculous to think of them as fit to teach, or do anything. Oh no; they have to go to Germany for a year – anyway, to somewhere for a year – and come back with whiskers and look like something.

I once put the question of shortening the college curriculum to my old friend Dean Elderberry Foible, dean of the Faculty of Arts. You didn't know him, but there was a dean at your college just like him. "Preposterous," he said, "preposterous!" And that settled it.

If we turn from the general view to the particular subjects, the case against any attempt to shorten the curriculum becomes simply overwhelming – so much so that we are crushed and humbled in presenting it. Imagine trying to leave out mathematics – the queen of sciences; or history – the very basis for understanding our modern life; or English literature – our legacy common to England and America, dear as the very hearthstones of our homes – who dares touch that?

Or who will dare disturb Latin, the bedrock of our culture; or foreign languages, the amenity of polite life; or geology, deep as the caverns of thought; biology, life's interpretation; or the social sciences, the key to the padlock of happiness still closed. Help! Nothing but pretentious ignorance could suggest leaving out anything. As to any shortening, ask again my friend Dean Elderberry Foible and he will tell you that you can't. "My dear sir, you may wish to, but you simply can't" – with that academic finality with which professors dismiss the ideas of students.

So it appears even to ourselves on a first survey. Take mathematics. How can you shorten the subject? That stern struggle with the multiplication table, for many people not yet ended in victory, how can you make it less? Square root, as obdurate as a hardwood stump in a pasture – nothing but years of effort can extract it. You can't hurry the process.

Or pass from arithmetic to algebra: you can't shoulder your way past quadratic equations or ripple through the binomial theorem. Indeed, the other way; your feet are impeded in the tangled growth, your pace slackens, you sink and fall somewhere near the binomial theorem with the calculus in sight on the horizon. So died, for each of us, still bravely fighting, our mathematical training; except only for a set of people called "mathematicians" – born so, like crooks. Yet would we leave mathematics out? No, we hold our cross.

Latin too: do you want your son to grow up not knowing what a *sine qua non* is, and who wrote Virgil's *Aeneid*? Then he not only needs the whole present curriculum but more! At present the student learns just enough Latin not to be able to read it; he stops short of the saturation point – just gets wet with it and no more.

But why recite the entire list? The same truth holds, for the academic profession, of every one of the subjects of the school and college course. The student is not saturated, when he ought really to be soaked.

A parallel resistance blocks the pathway leading to the professions. The idea of any immediate entry into them, for a young man just out of college is ridiculous. A hundred years ago a man just out of college looked as good as a coin fresh from the mint, a sickle from the whetstone. At twenty-seven he was a Member of Congress, had four or five children, owned three or four thousand dollars' worth of property in his own right – and owed five thousand dollars. But nowadays! Imagine trusting a serious case of illness to a young fellow of twenty-seven barely out of college, and till yesterday an interne in a hospital. Out of the question!

And, later, when at last his turn comes, it is but a brief acme of success, and then, all of a sudden, it seems people are saying, "He's too old for the job, losing his grip – in fact, he's nearly fifty." He's an "old doctor" – once a term of esteem and confidence but now equivalent to an "old horse."

Thus in our ill-fit world youth and age jostle and hurry one another together – too young and then too old. Those who follow gardening know that green peas are first too young to pick and then, overnight as it seems, too old to eat. So with our educated people. Homer long ago said, "As is the race of leaves, so is the race of men." Make it college graduates and garden peas and it still holds good.

How did all this come about? Our system of education arose out of the mediaeval Latin schools of the church. It still carries, like a fossil snake in a stone, the mark of its original structure. Not that this was the earliest kind of education. But the others were different. Greek education included music and dancing and what we call the arts. It was supposed to fit people to live. Mediaeval education was supposed to fit people to die. Any school-boy of today can still feel the effect of it.

Greek education was free from the problems that have beset our own. It didn't include the teaching of languages, the Greeks despising all foreigners as barbarians. It avoided everything "practical" like the plague, and would have regarded a professor of Engineering as a child of the devil, misusing truth. Mathematics, crippled by the want of symbols, became a sort of dream – intense, difficult and proudly without purpose. Greek education carried with it no "exams" and "tests" for entry to the professions. A Greek dentist didn't have to pass in Latin. He used a hammer.

Thus philosophy, "the love of knowledge," came into its own, in talk as endless as on the porch of a Kentucky country store.

"Scholars" would deny the truth of this summary and talk of Archimedes, the world's first engineer, and Hippocrates, its earliest physician. But the proof of what I say is that Archimedes found no followers and Hippocrates waited five hundred years for Galen. Scholars always see exceptions where a plain man sees an even surface. But even a billiard ball, if you look close enough, is all covered with bumps.

Our education, then, comes down to us from the schools of the Middle Ages. These were organized by the church and the first aim was piety, not competence; the goal was the reading of the Scriptures and by that the salvation of the soul. On this basis, Alfred the Great planned schools for Saxon England. So, too, in France did Charlemagne, who couldn't read or write and felt a religious admiration for those who could – the same as an oil magnate of today feels toward a university.

So presently the monastic schools arose, and from their oriel windows came forth among the elm trees the sound of Latin chants intoned by choristers; and in the silent scriptorium the light from a stained window fell on the quiet "copyist" rewriting, letter by letter, in pigment upon parchment, "In the beginning was the Word." Thus passed monastic life in its quiet transition to Eternity.

These were the earliest schools – secluded, scholarly – born ancient like the "old-fashioned" children of aging parents. For the date, place then anywhere in the four hundred years from Alfred and Charlemagne to the days of Oxford and Paris.

These later schools – Oxford, Paris, and such – came when study no longer taught people how to die and keep out of hell, but how to live, as lawyers – two ambitions with an obvious relationship. Law hatched out under the wings of the church, as a duck hatches under a hen, later to horrify its parent.

Here again the vertebrate structure is still seen in the rock. Lincoln's Inn and Grey's Inn were originally, in a sense, works of God, the defunct Doctors Commons till its end a spirituality. Law, in England at least, struggled long before it shook off the hand of ghostly guidance. Even now the connection between law and religion remains in the quantity of oaths by which the business of the law secures its righteousness.

So there came, then, such schools as Oxford and Paris, which seem to have been at first huge random gatherings of students – mediaeval exaggeration puts 30,000 at Oxford in pre-record days. They had, before printing, hardly any books, and no examinations. The curriculum ran to endless discussion – more Kentucky. These "disputations" begot "tests" and awards (degrees) and brought into the world that child of sin, the written examination. A few odd people like Roger Bacon began digging into black knowledge about gunpowder, and so forth, and got put into jail for it. The lamp of learning still fell only on the Kingdom of Light, with lawyers dancing in the shadow.

The curriculum of these schools, the bedrock on which ours still rests, was the famous trinity of study, the Trivium, which meant grammar, rhetoric and logic; to this was supplemented the four further studies called the Quadrivium – music, arithmetic, geometry and astronomy. All were based on the use of Latin; they comprehended the whole circuit of human knowledge, and the supreme purpose of it all was salvation. The monk Alcuin, who was Charlemagne's "specialist" in education, has described for us how he taught his students:

To some I administer the honey of the sacred writings; others I try to inebriate with the wine of the ancient classics. I begin the nourishment of some with the apples of grammatical subtlety. I strive to illuminate many by the arrangement of the stars, as from the painted roof of a lofty palace.

The whole extent of human knowledge was still within human comprehension. In our own day we meet men who think they "know it all." In the Middle Ages there were men who were sure they did. Of course, where knowledge ended superstition began, and that was infinite.

It was this curriculum which in the course of centuries has been expanded beyond recognition like the toad in Aesop that would be an ox. And still it has not burst. It drags along its huge amorphous outline, flabby as a dinosaur, over fifteen years of life.

Here is what happened to expand it. The revival of learning resuscitated Greek, a study forgotten by all but the Arabs. The rising kingdoms that replaced feudalism brought national States and set people to learning one another's languages. The English, having forgotten French, had to learn it again. Italian became "polite." Milton suggested that one ought to learn it, "in an odd hour." Modern languages were still not a part of education, but a sort of annex; so they remained till yesterday in England where all Englishmen were supposed to "know French" from a governess and a copy of Ollendorff's *Grammar* and a trip to Boulogne. But, till yesterday, Eton, Rugby and Oxford never heard of it.

Printing, once in real use, expanded both opportunity and obligation. Students henceforth had books. Contacts with the Arabs revealed a system of decimal notation that made arithmetic a reality and algebra a power. Mathematics in the time of the Stuarts, with logarithms and the calculus, ceased to be a dream. Physics converted Alcuin's wonder of the sky into classroom formulae.

But even though mathematics in the sixteen hundreds, in the days of Newton and Descartes, had become a real and intensive study – far transcending in reach and in difficulty anything within the range of the ordinary college man of today – it was still regarded rather as an annex to learning than as learning itself. The place of priority still lay with classical study, with the literature of Greece and Rome. In this America was a faithful child of England. Our earliest college education was stamped with Roman letters, and its passion for the Bible in the wilderness made it even revert somewhat to the mediaeval type. The rules that were promulgated in 1642 for admission to Harvard College lay down the qualification thus:—

When any scholar is able to understand Tully or such like classical Latin author extempore, *and to make and speak true Latin in verse and prose,* suo ut aiunt Marte: *and to decline perfectly the paradigms of nouns and verbs in the Greek tongue: let him then and not before be capable of admission into the college.*

For readers whose Latinity has slipped away from them, let it be explained that Tully is not Irish, but means Cicero. Earlier generations properly called Romans by their names, and not, as we have come to do, with many of them, by their nicknames. Tully was called "Cicero" (or bean-head) as one of us might be called "Shorty." Harvard Latin in 1642 was still undefiled.

On the terms indicated few of us now would get into Harvard. Fewer still would get out, since, for that, every scholar had to be

"found able to read the originals of the Old and New Testaments into the Latin tongue and to resolve them logically: withal being of godly life and conversation."

On the outside edge or fringe of the classical studies, of which mathematics and logic formed an adjunct, were such things as natural philosophy, destined to vast and rapid expansion, but of which the classical doctors of divinity remained ignorant.

By the time of Queen Anne, some scholars already admitted that they didn't know everything – not many, though, or at least they qualified it by saying that what they didn't know wasn't worth knowing.

What they referred to by this last phrase was this natural philosophy, the new range of knowledge that the eighteenth century was gathering, item by item, fact by fact. These grew into the sciences of life – botany and zoology, later to get their true name of biology. Reverend classical scholars, full to the throat with declensions, set them aside as a disturbance of the Book of Genesis. But they wouldn't down.

Beside them grew, equally despised by the classicists, the electric science drawn by Franklin from the clouds, the oxygen distilled by Priestley from water, the geology of Lyell, dug up from what was once called Hades. All the world knows the story. Within another hundred years a vast series of studies known as the natural sciences – at first opposed, derided and left to mechanics and steam-engine drivers – broke at last the barriers of the schools and flooded wide over the curriculum.

But the barriers, in England at least, did not break until the waters had risen high and the pressure had become overwhelming. In the middle nineteenth century, as Professor Huxley complained, the so-called public schools had still a curriculum of the Middle Ages.

Until a few years back [he wrote in 1893], a boy might have passed through any one of the great public schools with the greatest distinction and credit and might never so much as heard of modern geography, modern history and modern literature, of the English language as a language, or of the whole circle of the sciences, physical, moral and social; might never have heard that the earth goes round the sun; that England underwent a great revolution in 1688 and France another in 1789; that there once lived certain notable men called Chaucer, Shakespeare, Milton, Voltaire, Goethe, Schiller.

With this protest of common sense went a certain protest of spite – as against aristocratic culture by those unable to share it. Witness Herbert Spencer's diatribe against "The Education of a Gentleman."

Men dress their children's minds as they do their bodies

in the prevailing fashion. As the Orinoco Indian puts on his paint before he leaves his hut . . . so a boy's drilling in Latin and Greek is insisted on, not because of their intrinsic value, but that he may not be disgraced by being found ignorant of them – that he may have the education of a gentleman.

But when at last the barriers broke, the new science came in a flood, till every high school student, in America more even than in England, turned alchemist, and every class-room sputtered with electricity. And with this, in the colleges first and spreading downwards to the schools, came a still newer set of studies – the social studies, economics and politics, the mingled brood of happiness and despair, of progress and poverty that Mill and Spencer and such people let loose upon the world. So deeply have they spread that little children learn "civics" first and find out what it means after; and so widely that the Japanese have studied it from Europe and teach it to the Chinese.

And as if civics and social welfare were not enough for the already overburdened curriculum, a chariot creaking up the rough slope of Parnassus, "Business," in the form of schools of commerce, must needs leap on top of the load. It handed so heavy a tip to the driver that it could not be put off, and more than that it began to demand that the oldest and most respectable of the passengers be thrown out to make room for it.

So there we stand, or rather move slowly onward, the ascent of Parnassus turned into a ten years' journey during which the passengers must amuse themselves as best they may with the cards and dice of college activities.

Meantime it is only to be expected that the conditions of the journey react upon the minds of the passengers. In other words it is only natural that this vast burden of an increasing curriculum sets up a reaction in the minds of the pupil and the student. From their earliest years they become accustomed to reckon up the things that they have done and finished with. "We've finished Scripture," says a little girl in a child's school; "we had it last year." For her the mould of religious thought is all set. Don't ask her the names of the twelve Apostles. She's had them – last year. She is not responsible for the Apostles any more. So does the high school student count up his years still needed for matriculation as eagerly as a mariner measures his distance to the shore. The college student opens his career by classing himself not according to the year in which he enters but according to the year in which he hopes to get out. The class matriculating in 1940 call out in their infant breath, "Rah! Rah! Forty-four."

How strange it is, our little procession of life! The child says, "When I am a big boy." But what is that? The big boy says, "When I grow up." And then, grown up, he says, "When I get married." But to be married, what is that after all? The thought changes to "When I'm able to retire." And then, when retirement comes, he looks back over the landscape traversed; a cold wind seems to sweep over it; somehow he has missed it all, and it is gone. Life, we learn too late, is in the living, in the tissue of every day and hour. So it should be with education.

But so it is not; a false view discolours it all. For the vastly great part of it the student's one aim is to get done with it. There comes a glad time in his life when he has "finished" mathematics, a happy day when he has done philosophy, an exhilarating hour when he realizes that he is finished with "compulsory English." Then at last his four years are out, his sentence expired, and he steps out of college a free man, without a stain on his character – and not much on his mind. . . . Later on, he looks backs wistfully and realizes how different it might have been.

It is the purpose of this book in the chapters that follow to discuss this discrepancy between education and life. The field of education here discussed is that of "general education" and the liberal arts which occupy about twenty years of the life of the great majority of college students. The work of technical and professional schools – engineering, medicine and law – lies apart. Here the adaptation of the means to the end is sufficiently direct to lessen the danger of wandering into the wilderness as liberal arts has done.

This wandering into the wilderness has made the journey of education too long, too cumbersome and too expensive. Worse still, at the end of its wandering it comes to a full stop. The road comes to an end just when it ought to be getting somewhere. The passengers alight, shaken and weary, to begin, all over again, something else.

Humour as I See it

It is only fair that at the back of this book I should be allowed a few pages to myself to put down some things that I really think.

Until two weeks ago I might have taken my pen in hand to write about humour with the confident air of an acknowledged professional.

But that time is past. Such claim as I had has been taken from me. In fact I stand unmasked. An English reviewer writing in a literary journal, the very name of which is enough to put contradiction to sleep, has said of my writing, "What is there, after all, in Professor Leacock's humour but a rather ingenious mixture of hyberbole and myosis?"

The man was right. How he stumbled upon this trade secret I do not know. But I am willing to admit, since the truth is out, that it has long been my custom in preparing an article of a humorous nature to go down to the cellar and mix up half a gallon of myosis with a pint of hyperbole. If I want to give the article a decidedly literary character, I find it well to put in about half a pint of paresis. The whole thing is amazingly simple.

But I only mention this by way of introduction and to dispel any idea that I am conceited enough to write about humour, with the professional authority of Ella Wheeler Wilcox writing about love, or Eva Tanguay talking about dancing.

All that I dare claim is that I have as much sense of humour as other people. And, oddly enough, I notice that everybody else makes this same claim. Any man will admit, if need be, that his sight is not good, or that he cannot swim, or shoots badly with a rifle, but to touch upon his sense of humour is to give him a mortal affront.

"No," said a friend of mine the other day, "I never go to Grand Opera," and then he added with an air of pride, "You see, I have absolutely no ear for music."

"You don't say so!" I exclaimed.

"None!" he went on. "I can't tell one tune from another. I don't know *Home, Sweet Home* from *God Save the King*. I can't tell whether a man is tuning a violin or playing a sonata."

He seemed to get prouder and prouder over each item of his own deficiency. He ended by saying that he had a dog at his house that had a far better ear for music than he had. As soon as his wife or any visitor started to play the piano the dog always began to howl – plaintively, he said – as if it were hurt. He himself never did this.

When he had finished I made what I thought a harmless comment.

"I suppose," I said, "that you find your sense of humour deficient in the same way: the two generally go together."

My friend was livid with rage in a moment.

"Sense of humour!" he said. "My sense of humour! Me without a sense of humour! Why, I suppose I've a keener sense of humour than any man, or any two men, in this city!"

From that he turned to bitter personal attack. He said that *my* sense of humour seemed to have withered altogether.

He left me, still quivering with indignation.

Personally, however, I do not mind making the admission, however damaging it may be, that there are certain forms of so-called humour, or, at least, fun, which I am quite unable to appreciate. Chief among these is that ancient thing called the Practical Joke.

"You never knew McGann, did you?" a friend of mine asked me the other day.

When I said I had never known McGann, he shook his head with a sigh, and said:

"Ah, you should have known McGann. He had the greatest sense of humour of any man I ever knew – always full of jokes. I remember one night at the boarding-house where we were, he stretched a string across the passage-way and then rang the dinner bell. One of the boarders broke his leg. We nearly died laughing."

"Dear me!" I said. "What a humorist! Did he often do things like that?"

"Oh, yes, he was at them all the time. He used to put tar in the tomato soup, and beeswax and tin-tacks on the chairs. He was full of ideas. They seemed to come to him without any trouble."

McGann, I understand, is dead. I am not sorry for it. Indeed I think that for most of us the time has gone by when we can see the fun of putting tacks on chairs, or thistles in beds, or live snakes in people's boots.

To me it has always seemed that the very essence of good humour is that it must be without harm and without malice. I admit that there is in all of us a certain vein of the old original demoniacal humour or joy in the misfortune of another which sticks to us like our original sin. It ought not to be funny to see a man, especially a fat and pompous man, slip suddenly on a banana skin. But it is. When a skater on a pond who is describing graceful circles, and showing off before the crowd, breaks through the ice and gets a ducking, everybody shouts with joy. To the original savage, the cream of the joke in such cases was found if the man who slipped broke his neck, or the man who went through the ice never came up again. I can imagine a group of prehistoric men standing around the ice-hole where he had disappeared and laughing till their sides split. If there had been such a thing as a prehistoric newspaper, the affair would have been headed up: *"Amusing Incident. Unknown Gentleman Breaks Through Ice and Is Drowned."*

But our sense of humour under civilisation has been weakened. Much of the fun of this sort of thing has been lost on us.

Children, however, still retain a large share of this primitive sense of enjoyment.

I remember once watching two little boys making snowballs at the side of the street and getting ready a little store of them to use. As they worked, there came along an old man wearing a silk hat, and belonging by appearance to the class of "jolly old gentlemen." When he saw the boys his gold spectacles gleamed with kindly enjoyment. He began waving his arms and calling "Now, then, boys, free shot at me! free shot!" In his gaiety he had, without noticing it, edged himself over the sidewalk on to the street. An express cart collided with him and knocked him over on his back in a heap of snow. He lay there gasping and trying to get the snow off his face and spectacles. The boys gathered up their snow-balls and took a run toward him. "Free shot!" they yelled. "Soak him! Soak him!"

I repeat, however, that for me, as I suppose for most of us, it is a prime condition of humour that it must be without harm or malice, nor should it convey incidentally any real picture of sorrow or suffering or death. There is a great deal in the humour of Scotland (I admit its general merit) which seems to me, not being a Scotchman, to sin in this respect. Take this familiar story (I quote it as something already known and not for the sake of telling it).

A Scotchman had a sister-in-law – his wife's sister – with

whom he could never agree. He always objected to going anywhere with her, and in spite of his wife's entreaties always refused to do so. The wife was taken mortally ill and as she lay dying, she whispered, "John, ye'll drive Janet with you to the funeral, will ye no?" The Scotchman, after an internal struggle, answered, "Margaret, I'll do it for ye, but it'll spoil my day."

Whatever humour there may be in this is lost for me by the actual and vivid picture that it conjures up – the dying wife, the darkened room and the last whispered request.

No doubt the Scotch see things differently. That wonderful people – whom personally I cannot too much admire – always seem to me to prefer adversity to sunshine, to welcome the prospect of a pretty general damnation, and to live with grim cheerfulness within the very shadow of death. Alone among the nations they have converted the devil – under such names as Old Horny – into a familiar acquaintance not without a certain grim charm of his own. No doubt also there enters into their humour something of the original barbaric attitude towards things. For a primitive people who saw death often and at first hand, and for whom the future world was a vivid reality that could be *felt*, as it were, in the midnight forest and heard in the roaring storm, it was no doubt natural to turn the flank of terror by forcing a merry and jovial acquaintance with the unseen world. Such a practice as a wake, and the merry-making about the corpse, carry us back to the twilight of the world, with the poor savage in his bewildered misery, pretending that his dead still lived. Our funeral with its black trappings and its elaborate ceremonies is the lineal descendant of a merry-making. Our undertaker is, by evolution, a genial master of ceremonies, keeping things lively at the death-dance. Thus have the ceremonies and the trappings of death been transformed in the course of the ages till the forced gaiety is gone, and the black hearse and the gloomy mutes betoken the cold dignity of our despair.

But I fear this article is getting serious. I must apologise.

I was about to say, when I wandered from the point, that there is another form of humour which I am also quite unable to appreciate. This is that particular form of story which may be called, *par excellence*, the English Anecdote. It always deals with persons of rank and birth, and except for the exalted nature of the subject itself, is, as far as I can see, absolutely pointless.

This is the kind of thing that I mean.

"His Grace the Fourth Duke of Marlborough was noted

for the open-handed hospitality which reigned at Blenheim, the family seat, during his regime. One day on going in to luncheon it was discovered that there were thirty guests present, whereas the table only held covers for twenty-one. 'Oh, well,' said the Duke, not a whit abashed, 'some of us will have to eat standing up.' Everybody, of course, roared with laughter."

My only wonder is that they didn't kill themselves with it. A mere roar doesn't seem enough to do justice to such a story as this.

The Duke of Wellington has been made the storm-centre of three generations of wit of this sort. In fact the typical Duke of Wellington story has been reduced to a thin skeleton such as this:

"A young subaltern once met the Duke of Wellington coming out of Westminster Abbey. 'Good morning, your Grace,' he said, 'rather a wet morning.' 'Yes,' said the Duke, with a very rigid bow, 'but it was a damn sight wetter, sir, on the morning of Waterloo.' The young subaltern, rightly rebuked, hung his head."

Nor is it only the English who sin in regard to anecdotes.

One can indeed make the sweeping assertion that the telling of stories as a mode of amusing others ought to be kept within strict limits. Few people realise how extremely difficult it is to tell a story so as to reproduce the real fun of it – to "get it over" as the actors say. The mere "facts" of a story seldom make it funny. It needs the right words, with every word in its proper place. Here and there, perhaps once in a hundred times, a story turns up which needs no telling. The humour of it turns so completely on a sudden twist or incongruity in the *dénouement* of it that no narrator, however clumsy, can altogether fumble it.

Take, for example, this well-known instance – a story which, in one form or other, everybody has heard.

"George Grossmith, the famous comedian, was once badly run down and went to consult a doctor. It happened that the doctor, though, like everybody else, he had often seen Grossmith on the stage, had never seen him without his make-up and did not know him by sight. He examined his patient, looked at his tongue, felt his pulse and tapped his lungs. Then he shook his head. 'There's nothing wrong with you, sir,' he said, 'except that you're run down from overwork and worry. You need rest and amusement. Take a night off and go and see George Grossmith at the Savoy.' 'Thank you,' said the patient, 'I *am* George Grossmith.' "

Let the reader please observe that I have purposely told this story all wrongly, just as wrongly as could be, and yet there is something left of it. Will the reader kindly look back to the beginning of it and see for himself just how it ought to be narrated and what obvious error has been made? If he has any particle of the artist in his make-up, he will see at once that the story ought to begin:

"One day a very haggard and nervous-looking patient called at the house of a fashionable doctor, etc. etc."

In other words, the chief point of the joke lies in keeping it concealed till the moment when the patient says, "Thank you, I am George Grossmith." But the story is such a good one that it cannot be completely spoiled even when told wrongly. This particular anecdote has been variously told of George Grossmith, Coquelin, Joe Jefferson, John Hare, Cyril Maude, and about sixty others. And I have noticed that there is a certain type of man who, on hearing this story about Grossmith, immediately tells it all back again, putting in the name of somebody else, and goes into new fits of laughter over it, as if the change of name made it brand new.

But few people, I repeat, realise the difficulty of reproducing a humorous or comic effect in its original spirit.

"I saw Harry Lauder last night," said Griggs, a Stock Exchange friend of mine, as we walked up town together the other day. "He came on to the stage in kilts" (here Griggs started to chuckle) "and he had a slate under his arm" (here Griggs began to laugh quite heartily), "and he said, 'I always like to carry a slate with me' (of course he said it in Scotch but I can't do the Scotch the way he does) 'just in case there might be any figures I'd be wanting to put down'" (by this time, Griggs was almost suffocated with laughter) – "and he took a little bit of chalk out of his pocket, and he said" (Griggs was now almost hysterical), "'I like to carry a wee bit chalk along because I find the slate is'" (Griggs was now faint with laughter) "'the slate is – is – not much good without the chalk.'"

Griggs had to stop, with his hand to his side, and lean against a lamp-post. "I can't, of course, do the Scotch the way Harry Lauder does it," he repeated.

Exactly. He couldn't do the Scotch and he couldn't do the rich mellow voice of Mr. Lauder and the face beaming with merriment, and the spectacles glittering with amusement, and he couldn't do the slate, nor the "wee bit chalk" – in fact he couldn't do any of it. He ought merely to save said, "Harry

Lauder," and leaned up against a post and laughed till he had got over it.

Yet in spite of everything, people insist on spoiling conversation by telling stories. I know nothing more dreadful at a dinner table than one of these amateur raconteurs – except perhaps two of them. After about three stories have been told, there falls on the dinner table an uncomfortable silence, in which everybody is aware that everybody else is trying hard to think of another story, and is failing to find it. There is no peace in the gathering again till some man of firm and quiet mind turns to his neighbour and says. "But after all there is no doubt that whether we like it or not prohibition is coming." Then everybody in his heart says, "Thank heaven!" and the whole tableful are happy and contented again, till one of the story-tellers "thinks of another," and breaks loose.

Worst of all perhaps is the modest story-teller who is haunted by the idea that one has heard this story before. He attacks you after this fashion:

"I heard a very good story the other day on the steamer going to Bermuda" – then he pauses with a certain doubt in his face – "but perhaps you've heard this?"

"No, no, I've never been to Bermuda. Go ahead."

"Well, this is a story that they tell about a man who went down to Bermuda one winter to get cured of rheumatism – but you've heard this?"

"No, no."

"Well he had rheumatism pretty bad and he went to Bermuda to get cured of it. And so when he went into the hotel he said to the clerk at the desk – but, perhaps you know this."

"No, no, go right ahead."

"Well, he said to the clerk, 'I want a room that looks out over the sea' – but perhaps –"

Now the sensible thing to do is to stop the narrator right at this point. Say to him quietly and firmly, "Yes, I have heard that story. I always liked it ever since it came out in *Tit Bits* in 1878, and I read it every time I see it. Go on and tell it to me and I'll sit back with my eyes closed and enjoy it."

No doubt the story-telling habit owes much to the fact that ordinary people, quite unconsciously, rate humour very low: I mean, they underestimate the difficulty of "making humour." It would never occur to them that the thing is hard, meritorious and dignified. Because the result is gay and light, they think the process must be. Few people would realise that it is much harder to write one of Owen Seaman's "funny" poems in *Punch* than to write one of the Archbishop of Canterbury's sermons. Mark Twain's *Huckleberry Finn* is a greater work than Kant's *Critique of Pure Reason,* and Charles Dickens's creation of Mr. Pickwick did more for the elevation of the human race – I say it in all seriousness – than Cardinal Newman's *Lead, Kindly Light, Amid the Encircling Gloom.* Newman only cried out for light in the gloom of a sad world. Dickens gave it.

But the deep background that lies behind and beyond what we call humour is revealed only to the few who, by instinct or by effort, have given thought to it. The world's humour, in its best and greatest sense, is perhaps the highest product of our civilisation. One thinks here not of the mere spasmodic effects of the comic artist or the blackface expert of the vaudeville show, but of the really great humour which, once or twice in a generation at best, illuminates and elevates our literature. It is no longer dependent upon the mere trick and quibble of words, or the odd and meaningless incongruities in things that strike us as "funny." Its basis lies in the deeper contrasts offered by life itself: the strange incongruity between our aspiration and our achievement, the eager and fretful anxieties of to-day that fade into nothingness to-morrow, the burning pain and the sharp sorrow that are softened in the gentle retrospect of time, till as we look back upon the course that has been traversed we pass in view the panorama of our lives, as people in old age may recall, with mingled tears and smiles, the angry quarrels of their childhood. And here, in its larger aspect, humour is blended with pathos till the two are one, and represent, as they have in every age, the mingled heritage of tears and laughter that is our lot on earth.

When Men Retire

My old friend Mr. McPherson retired from the flour and feed business – oh, quite a few years ago. He said it was time to get out and give young Charlie a chance – even then "young Charlie" was getting near fifty. Anyway old Mr. McPherson said he wasn't going to keep his nose to the grindstone for ever.

I don't mean that he absolutely dropped out of the business; but, as he himself said, he took it easy. The McPhersons had a fine business, two or three big mills and a central office in our home town. Always, before he retired, Mr. McPherson would be down at the office sharp at eight – the flour and feed is an early business. When he retired he gave all that up. He'd loaf in anywhere round ten minutes past, or sometimes even twenty. It was the same way after lunch – or at least I mean after "dinner"; they don't have "lunch" in the flour and feed business; they have dinner at noon. After dinner if Mr. McPherson didn't feel like getting up and walking to the office at one o'clock, he'd drive down in a cab. And at five o'clock, when the office closed, if he didn't feel like going home right away, he'd stay for a while and run over some of the day's invoices. Or perhaps, if he felt like it, he'd go over to the mill, because the mill didn't close till six, and just fool around there a while helping the men bag up some of the farmers' orders.

One thing, though, that Mr. McPherson insists on, now that he's retired, is that, as he himself says, he never interferes. The business, as he explains, belongs now to the children. That means young Charlie and Lavinia – bless me! Lavinia must be not far from sixty; she keeps the house. To those two and a married daughter in Scotland. The old man has never transferred the business in any legal sense. He says it isn't necessary as long as he's alive. But it's *theirs* just the same, and he tells them so. And, as I say, he doesn't interfere; "young Charlie" is the general manager, and all his father does is just to look over the contracts to see what's doing, and keep an eye on the produce market to advise young Charlie when to buy – but only, mind you, to advise.

What's more, as Mr. McPherson himself loves to explain, he's not like a man who can't cut loose from business and enjoy himself. Oh, my no! Every year there's the St. Andrews dinner in the Odd Fellows' Hall, regular as clock-work, and every year Burns' birthday, when a few of them get together and have a big old time and read Burns out loud. And only four years ago Mr. McPherson took a trip to Scotland and saw his married daughter and Burns' grave and the big flour mills at Dumbarton, and paid for it all out of a commission on No. 1 wheat. Oh, no, Mr. McPherson says he never regrets his retirement: he can't think what it would be like to be back in harness.

My friend McAlpin was a banker – assistant general manager of a bank. He retired in the natural, normal course of things in accordance with the bank regulations. He made no plan or preparation for retirement. He said that it was enough for him to be rid of the strain of work. He'd have his mind free. So he would have had, if it hadn't happened that, on his first morning of retirement, as he walked down town, he felt a sort of wheeziness, a kind of, well, not exactly a pain, but a sort of compression. Anyway, a druggist gave him some bicarbonate of bismuth – he's told me about it himself ever so many times – or was it bisulphate of something? Anyway it fixed McAlpin up all right but it left him with a sort of feeling of flatulence, or flobbulence (he's explained it to me) that bothered him all morning till a friend told him to drink Vichy water, two or three quarts at a time. Now as a matter of fact you see, McAlpin had had that wheeziness every morning for years back when he went to the bank. But as soon as he opened the mail and began dictating, the wheeziness vanished, and the flobbulence never started. But the moment he retired, the wheeziness brought on the flobbulence; and Vichy water is all right, but there's so much chalk in it that if you take it you must follow it with an anticalcide of some sort. I don't know the names, But McAlpin has told me about them – bigusphate of carbon or any other antiscorbutic.

In fact, as McAlpin tells me, he has come to realize that his diet while he was in the bank was all wrong. He used to take bacon and eggs for breakfast, whereas now that he has looked into things he finds that bacon has no food value at all – contains no postulates. Eggs would be all right if taken with a germicide, but they lack vitamins. So what McAlpin eats now – he tells me this himself – is a proper balance of protein and carbohydrates.

McAlpin spends a good deal of his time in the drug stores. He says those fellows know a lot. Do you realize that if you take a drink of mineral water every half hour, with a touch of salt in it, it keeps your sebaceous glands open?

When McAlpin takes a holiday he goes down to Nuggett Springs where the thermal baths are. It's a new place and he says that they say that the doctors say that the water has a lower alkali content than any other. That's why he goes there, for the low alkali content. You take a bath every hour and in between you drink the water and the rest of the time you sit in it. McAlpin says that when he comes back he feels a hundred per cent more crustaceous that he did before. He attributes this to phosphorus.

My friend Tharpe, who was in Iron and Steel, retired to Paris. He retired at fifty-eight. He said he wanted to retire while he was still fresh enough to enjoy life – feel those muscles. He wanted to have a little fun in life, before he sank into old age. So he went over to Paris to have, as he himself so fervently put it, "a whale of a time."

I saw him there six months later, in a night-supper restaurant. He had with him something that looked like an odelisk – isn't that the word? – anyway something Moorish with slanting eyes and a crescent diadem. Tharpe came over and spoke to me. He looked like a boiled lobster, all red and black. He said he felt fine. He said he was just starting out for the evening. He felt, he said, A.1.

I saw him in the hotel next morning. He was in the barber shop. The barber was fixing him up. He looked about four colors, mostly black and yellow. He said he felt great. The barber was steaming him, boiling him and squirting things over him. Then he went up to the drug store and the druggist "fixed him" – washed him right out – and then into the bar and the bartender "fixed him" – toned him right up with a couple of "eye-openers." Then he started off. He had on a pongee suit and a panama hat and a French silk tie, and he looked pretty slick, but battered. He said he felt fine. He said he was going out to play baccarat with two men he met the night before – Russians – he couldn't remember their names – Sonovitch or Dombroski or something. Anyway one of them was a cousin of the Czar. He said he felt elegant.

Tharpe is in a home just now, in England – a rest home. He's taking the rest cure, and then he is to take the gold cure and after that a brain cure. A big English doctor took out part of his skull. He says he feels A.1. He has lost most of his money and he's coming back to the Iron and Steel business. He says it beats Paris.

A peculiarly interesting case of retirement has been that of my long-time friend the Senior Professor of Greek at the college here. When he retired the Chancellor of the University said at the Convocation that our regret at Professor Dim's retirement was tempered by the fact that we realized that he would now be able to complete the studies on Homer's *Odyssey* which had occupied him for so many years. Notice, to *complete*. The general supposition was that in all these long years, in all the evenings of his spare time he'd been working on Homer's *Odyssey*, and that now all that he needed was a little time and breathing space and the brilliant studies would be consolidated into a book. To *complete* – and I was the only one who knew that he hadn't even started. He had begun, ever so many years ago, when we were fellow juniors, talking of Homer's *Odyssey*. There was something he wanted to do about it – I forget just what; either to prove that there was never any Homer or that there was never any Odyssey. At any rate it was one of those big academic problems that professors select as a life work. It began to be understood that he was "working on Homer's *Odyssey*"; then that he was doing a book on Homer's *Odyssey*, and then that he had nearly done it, and only needed time to *complete* it. And all that time he hadn't started. Professors are like that.

The years go by so easily – Commencement Day and a new session – you can't begin anything then – mid-session, impossible – final exams and the end of the session – out of the question to start anything then; a man must rest sometime. And you don't start Homer in the long vacation on the coast of Maine.

So when Professor Dim retired, people on the street would stop him and ask, "How's the book coming on?" And he could only turn pink and gurgle something. I'm the only one who knows that he hasn't started it. He's been getting pretty frail the last two winters; some of his old pupils sent him south last winter, so that he could finish his book. He didn't. They gave him a trip up north last summer – but not far enough. They talk now of sending him to Greece where the *Odyssey* began. They're afraid, some of them – this, of course, they say very gently and kindly – they're afraid that the old fellow may not live to finish the book. I know that he won't. He hasn't started.

But as to this retirement business, let me give a word of advice to all of you young fellows round fifty. Some of you have been talking of it and even looking forward to it. Have nothing to do with it. Listen; it's like this. Have you ever been out for a late autumn walk in the closing part of the afternoon, and suddenly looked up to realize that the leaves have practically all gone? You hadn't realized it. And you notice that the sun has set already, the day gone before you knew it – and with that a cold wind blows across the landscape. That's retirement.

L'envoi.
The Train to
Mariposa

It leaves the city every day about five o'clock in the evening, the train for Mariposa.

Strange that you did not know of it, though you come from the little town – or did, long years ago.

Odd that you never knew, in all these years, that the train was there every afternoon puffing up steam in the city station, and that you might have boarded it any day and gone home. No, not "home" – of course you couldn't call it "home" now; "home" means that big red sandstone house of yours in the costlier part of the city. "Home" means, in a way, this Mausoleum Club where you sometimes talk with me of the times that you had as a boy in Mariposa.

But of course "home" would hardly be the word you would apply to the little town, unless perhaps, late at night, when you'd been sitting reading in a quiet corner somewhere such a book as the present one.

Naturally you don't know of the Mariposa train now. Years ago, when you first came to the city as a boy with your way to make, you knew of it well enough, only too well. The price of a ticket counted in those days, and though you knew of the train you couldn't take it, but sometimes from sheer homesickness you used to wander down to the station on a Friday afternoon after your work, and watch the Mariposa people getting on the train and wish that you could go.

Why, you knew that train at one time better, I suppose, than any other single thing in the city, and loved it too for the little town in the sunshine that it ran to.

Do you remember how when you first began to make money you used to plan that just as soon as you were rich, really rich, you'd go back home again to the little town and build a great big house with a fine verandah – no stint about it, the best that money could buy, planed lumber, every square foot of it, and a fine picket fence in front of it.

It was to be one of the grandest and finest houses that thought could conceive; much finer, in true reality, than that vast palace of sandstone with the porte-cochère and the sweeping conservatories that you afterwards built in the costlier part of the city.

But if you have half forgotten Mariposa, and long since lost the way to it, you are only like the greater part of the men here in this Mausoleum Club in the city. Would you believe it that practically every one of them came from Mariposa once upon a time, and that there isn't one of them that doesn't sometimes dream in the dull quiet of the long evening here in the club, that some day he will go back and see the place.

They all do. Only they're half ashamed to own it.

Ask your neighbour there at the next table whether the partridge that they sometimes serve to you here can be compared for a moment to the birds that he and you, or he and someone else, used to shoot as boys in the spruce thickets along the lake. Ask him if he ever tasted duck that could for a moment be compared to the black ducks in the rice marsh along the Ossawippi. And as for fish, and fishing – no, don't ask him about that, for if he ever starts telling you of the chub they used to catch below the mill dam and the green bass that used to lie in the water-shadow of the rocks beside the Indian's Island, not even the long dull evening in this club would be long enough for the telling of it.

But no wonder they don't know about the five o'clock train for Mariposa. Very few people know about it. Hundreds of them know that there is a train that goes out at five o'clock, but they mistake it. Ever so many of them think it's just a suburban train. Lots of people that take it every day think it's only the train to the golf grounds, but the joke is that after it passes out of the city and the suburbs and the golf grounds, it turns itself little by little into the Mariposa train thundering and pounding towards the north with hemlock sparks pouring out into the darkness from the funnel of it.

Of course you can't tell it just at first. All those people that are crowding into it with golf clubs, and wearing knickerbockers and flat caps, would deceive anybody. That crowd of suburban people going home on commutation tickets and sometimes standing thick in the aisles, those are, of course, not Mariposa people. But look round a little bit and you'll find them easily enough. Here and there in the crowd those people with the clothes that are perfectly all right and yet look odd in some way, the women with the peculiar hats and the – what do you say? – last year's fashions? Ah yes, of course, that must be it.

Anyway, those are the Mariposa people all right enough. That man with the two-dollar panama and the glaring spectacles is one of the greatest judges that ever adorned the bench of Missinaba County. That clerical gentleman with the wide black hat, who is explaining to the man with him the marvellous mechanism of the new air brake (one of the most conspicuous illustrations of the divine structure of the physical universe), surely you have seen him before. Mariposa people! Oh yes, there are any number of them on the train every day.

But of course you hardly recognize them while the train is still passing through the suburbs and the golf district and the outlying parts of the city area. But wait a little, and you will see that when the city is well behind you, bit by bit the train changes its character. The electric locomotive that took you through the city tunnels is off now and the old wood engine is hitched on in its place. I suppose, very probably, you haven't seen one of these wood engines since you were a boy forty years ago – the old engine with a wide top like a hat on its funnel, and with sparks enough to light up a suit for damages once in every mile.

Do you see, too, that the trim little cars that came out of the city on the electric suburban express are being discarded now at the way stations, one by one, and in their place is the old familiar car with the stuff cushions in red plush (how gorgeous it once seemed!) and with a box stove set up in one end of it? The stove is burning furiously at its sticks this autumn evening, for the air sets in chill as you get clear away from the city and are rising up to the higher ground of the country of the pines and the lakes.

Look from the window as you go. The city is far behind now and right and left of you there are trim farms with elms and maples near them and with tall windmills beside the barns that you can still see in the gathering dusk. There is a dull red light from the windows of the farmstead. It must be comfortable there after the roar and clatter of the city, and only think of the still quiet of it.

As you sit back half dreaming in the car, you keep wondering why it is that you never came up before in all these years. Ever so many times you planned that just as soon as the rush and strain of business eased up a little, you would take the train and go back to the little town to see what it was like now, and if things had changed much since your day. But each time when your holidays came, somehow you changed your mind and went down to Narragansett or

Nagahuckett or Nagasomething, and left over the visit to Mariposa for another time.

It is almost night now. You can still see the trees and the fences and the farmsteads, but they are fading fast in the twilight. They have lengthened out the train by this time with a string of flat cars and freight cars between where we are sitting and the engine. But at every crossway we can hear the long muffled roar of the whistle, dying to a melancholy wail that echoes into the woods; the woods, I say, for the farms are thinning out and the track plunges here and there into great stretches of bush – tall tamarack and red scrub willow and with a tangled undergrowth of brush that has defied for two generations all attempts to clear it into the form of fields.

Why, look, that great space that seems to open out in the half-dark of the falling evening – why, surely yes, Lake Ossawippi, the big lake, as they used to call it, from which the river runs down to the smaller lake – Lake Wissanotti – where the town of Mariposa has lain waiting for you there for thirty years.

This is Lake Ossawippi surely enough. You would know it anywhere by the broad, still, black water with hardly a ripple, and with the grip of the coming frost already on it. Such a great sheet of blackness it looks as the train thunders along the side, swinging the curve of the embankment at a breakneck speed as it rounds the corner of the lake.

How fast the train goes this autumn night! You have travelled, I know you have, in the Empire State Express, and the New Limited and the Maritime Express that holds the record of six hundred whirling miles from Paris to Marseilles. But what are they to this, this mad career, this breakneck speed, this thundering roar of the Mariposa local driving hard to its home! Don't tell me that the speed is only twenty-five miles an hour. I don't care what it is. I tell you, and you can prove it for yourself if you will, that that train of mingled flat cars and coaches that goes tearing into the night, its engine whistle shrieking out its warning into the silent woods and echoing over the dull still lake, is the fastest train in the whole world.

Yes, and the best too – the most comfortable, the most reliable, the most luxurious and the speediest train that ever turned a wheel.

And the most genial, the most sociable too. See how the passengers all turn and talk to one another now as they get nearer and nearer to the little town. That dull reserve that seemed to hold the passengers in the electric suburban has clean vanished and gone. They are talking – listen – of the harvest, and the late election, and of how the local member is mentioned for the cabinet and all the old familiar topics of the sort. Already the conductor has changed his glazed hat for an ordinary round Christie and you can hear the passengers calling him and the brakeman "Bill" and "Sam" as if they were all one family.

What is it now – nine thirty? Ah, then we must be nearing the town – this big bush that we are passing through, you remember it surely as the great swamp just this side of the bridge over the Ossawippi? There is the bridge itself, and the long roar of the train as it rushes sounding over the trestle work that rises above the marsh. Hear the clatter as we pass the semaphores and the switch lights! We must be close in now!

What? it feels nervous and strange to be coming here again after all these years? It must indeed. No, don't bother to look at the reflection of your face in the window-pane shadowed by the night outside. Nobody could tell you now after all these years. Your face has changed in these long years of money-getting in the city. Perhaps if you had come back now and again, just at odd times, it wouldn't have been so.

There – you hear it? – the long whistle of the locomotive, one, two, three! You feel the sharp slackening of the train as it swings round the curve of the last embankment that brings it to the Mariposa station. See, too, as we round the curve, the row of the flashing lights, the bright windows of the depôt.

How vivid and plain it all is. Just as it used to be thirty years ago. There is the string of the hotel buses drawn up all ready for the train, and as the train rounds in and stops hissing and panting at the platform, you can hear above all other sounds the cry of the brakemen and the porters:

"MARIPOSA! MARIPOSA!"

And, as we listen, the cry grows fainter and fainter in our ears and we are sitting here again in the leather chairs of the Mausoleum Club, talking of the little Town in the Sunshine that once we knew.